Taste of Home's
Garden-Fresh Recipes

PICTURED ABOVE AND ON THE COVER: Tomato French Bread Lasagna (p. 43), Fruity Chili Sauce (p. 44), Herbed Cherry Tomatoes (p. 44) and Tomato Dill Soup (p. 43).

Produce-Packed Cookbook Is Pick of the Crop!

THE LONG HOURS of planting, watering and weeding have paid off...your backyard garden is ripe for the picking...and more picking.

Finding creative ways to put a bountiful harvest of homegrown fruits and vegetables to use can be a challenge. Well, drop the shovel, and dig into *Taste of Home's Garden-Fresh Recipes* instead. This recipe collection is full of 211 fresh ideas for soups and salads, main dishes, desserts and more, all calling for ingredients straight from the garden, fruit tree or berry patch.

Fellow gardeners from across the country shared these great recipes, which have appeared in past issues of *Taste of Home*

magazine and its "sister" publications.

Even if you don't have a green thumb, the plentiful supply of fresh produce available at farmers markets and supermarkets throughout the year guarantees you'll turn to the pages of this cookbook regardless of the season.

Before you fill a bushel basket, though, check out the "Guide to Vegetables" beginning on page 102. There you'll find all you need to know about picking (or buying), storing, preparing and cooking the fresh crops featured in this cookbook.

With *Taste of Home's Garden-Fresh Recipes* in your hands, you'll soon be harvesting a bounty of compliments!

Editor: Jean Steiner
Art Directors: Catherine Fletcher, Kathy Crawford
Senior Editor/Books: Heidi Reuter Lloyd
Associate Editor: Beth Wittlinger
Food Editor: Janaan Cunningham
Associate Food Editors: Coleen Martin, Diane Werner
Senior Recipe Editor: Sue A. Jurack
Recipe Editor: Janet Briggs
Editorial Assistant: Barb Czysz
Food Photography: Rob Hagen, Dan Roberts
Food Photography Artists: Julie Ferron, Sue Myers
Photo Studio Manager: Anne Schimmel
Senior Vice President, Editor in Chief: Catherine Cassidy
President: Barbara Newton
Chairman and Founder: Roy Reiman

Contents

Asparagus Puff Ring
Asparagus Mornay

Chapter 1
Asparagus

Asparagus Mornay
(Pictured at left)

Growing up on my parents' farm, we had a large asparagus patch. I still love asparagus, but my husband and kids weren't eager to eat it until I found this recipe.
—Linda McKee, Big Prairie, Ohio

1-1/2 pounds fresh asparagus, trimmed
1 tablespoon butter
1 tablespoon all-purpose flour
1 cup half-and-half cream
1/2 teaspoon chicken bouillon granules
1/8 teaspoon ground nutmeg
1/8 teaspoon salt
1/2 cup shredded Swiss cheese
2 tablespoons crushed butter-flavored
crackers

In a skillet, cook asparagus in a small amount of water until crisp-tender, about 6-8 minutes; drain. Arrange spears in the bottom of a greased 1-1/2-qt. baking dish; set aside and keep warm.

In a small saucepan, melt butter over low heat. Add flour; cook and stir for 1 minute. Whisk in the cream, bouillon, nutmeg and salt; bring to a boil over medium heat. Cook and stir for 2 minutes. Remove from the heat; stir in cheese until melted. Pour over asparagus. Sprinkle with cracker crumbs. Broil 6 in. from the heat for 3-5 minutes or until lightly browned. **Yield:** 4-6 servings.

Asparagus Puff Ring
(Pictured at left)

Every spring when I make this entree, I'm struck by how impressive it looks. Ham and asparagus in a creamy sauce are piled high in a cream puff shell.
—Shirley DeLange, Bryon Center, Michigan

3/4 cup water
6 tablespoons butter
3/4 cup all-purpose flour
1/2 teaspoon salt

3 eggs
1/4 cup grated Parmesan cheese, *divided*
FILLING:
1 pound fresh asparagus, cut into 1-inch
pieces
1/4 cup diced onion
2 tablespoons butter
2 tablespoons all-purpose flour
1/2 teaspoon salt
1/4 teaspoon pepper
1-1/2 cups milk
1/2 cup shredded Swiss cheese
2 tablespoons grated Parmesan cheese
2 cups diced fully cooked ham

In a saucepan over medium heat, bring water and butter to a boil. Add flour and salt all at once; stir until a smooth ball forms. Remove from heat; let stand for 5 minutes. Add eggs, one at a time, beating well after each; beat until smooth. Stir in 3 tablespoons Parmesan cheese.

Using 1/4 cupfuls of dough, form a ring around the sides of a greased 10-in. quiche pan or pie plate (mounds should touch). Top with the remaining cheese. Bake at 400° for 35 minutes.

Meanwhile, cook asparagus until crisp-tender, 3-4 minutes; drain. In a saucepan, saute onion in butter until tender. Stir in flour, salt and pepper. Gradually add milk; bring to a boil over medium heat, stirring constantly. Reduce heat; stir in cheeses until melted. Stir in ham and asparagus; spoon into ring. Serve immediately. **Yield:** 6 servings.

Asparagus Tips

For a quick and easy side dish, drizzle olive oil over trimmed fresh asparagus spears, sprinkle with salt and bake at 450° for 10-20 minutes, depending on the thickness of the asparagus spears.   —Lisa Hunn Barber
Lansdale, Pennsylvania

When grilling asparagus, use a grill rack to prevent thin spears from falling into the coals.   —Cheryl Shaw, Lafayette, Indiana

Asparagus Ham Swirls

(Pictured below)

I came across the recipe for this hot appetizer years ago and have made it many times to share with friends and co-workers. Asparagus, ham and cheese combine into a fun finger food. —Nancy Ingersol
Midlothian, Illinois

    16 fresh asparagus spears, trimmed
     3 tablespoons Dijon mustard
    16 thin slices fully cooked ham
    16 slices process Swiss cheese
     2 eggs, beaten
     1 cup dry bread crumbs
Vegetable oil

In a skillet, cook asparagus in a small amount of water until crisp-tender, about 6-8 minutes; drain well. Spread 1 teaspoon of mustard on each ham slice. Top with one slice of cheese. Place an asparagus spear at one end (trim to fit if needed). Roll up each ham slice tightly; secure with three toothpicks. Dip ham rolls in egg, then roll in bread crumbs.

In an electric skillet, heat 1 in. of oil to 350°. Fry rolls, a few at a time, until golden brown, about 3-4 minutes. Drain on paper towels; keep warm. Cut each roll between the toothpicks into three pieces. **Yield:** 4 dozen.

Oriental Asparagus Salad

A delightful change of pace from hot vegetable side dishes, this lovely asparagus salad gets an Oriental twist with a simple marinade and sesame seeds. Once you try it, you'll serve it time and again.
—Linda Hutton, Hayden, Idaho

Asparagus Ham Swirls

     1 pound fresh asparagus, cut into 2-inch
         pieces
     2 tablespoons soy sauce
     1 tablespoon vegetable oil
     1 tablespoon vinegar
 1-1/2 teaspoons sugar
     1 teaspoon sesame seeds, toasted
 1/4 to 1/2 teaspoon ground ginger
   1/4 teaspoon ground cumin

In a saucepan, cook the asparagus in a small amount of water until crisp-tender, about 3-4 minutes. Drain well and place in a large bowl.

Combine the soy sauce, oil, vinegar, sugar, sesame seeds, ginger and cumin; pour over asparagus and toss to coat. Cover and chill for 1 hour. Drain before serving. **Yield:** 4 servings.

Asparagus with Pimientos

This lovely, simple-to-prepare spring dish highlights the asparagus rather than hides it. The delicate topping of Parmesan cheese and bread crumbs complements the asparagus flavor and looks impressive.
—Adeline Piscitelli, Sayreville, New Jersey

     1 pound fresh asparagus, trimmed
   1/4 cup dry bread crumbs
     3 tablespoons butter
     2 tablespoons grated Parmesan cheese
     2 tablespoons chopped pimientos

In a saucepan over medium heat, cook asparagus in boiling salted water until tender, about 8 minutes. Meanwhile, in a skillet, brown bread crumbs in butter. Drain asparagus; place in a serving dish. Sprinkle with crumbs, cheese and pimientos. **Yield:** 4-6 servings.

Cream of Asparagus Soup

It's not difficult to fix a batch of this smooth, comforting soup. It has wonderful homemade goodness that warms me up. —Veva Hepler
Walla Walla, Washington

   1/2 cup chopped onion
     1 tablespoon vegetable oil
     2 cans (14-1/2 ounces *each*) chicken broth
 2-1/2 pounds fresh asparagus, trimmed and
         cut into 1-inch pieces
   1/4 teaspoon dried tarragon
   1/4 cup butter
   1/4 cup all-purpose flour

1/2 teaspoon salt
1/4 teaspoon white pepper
3 cups half-and-half cream
1-1/2 teaspoons lemon juice
Shredded Swiss cheese

In a large saucepan over medium heat, saute onion in oil until tender. Add broth, asparagus and tarragon; simmer until asparagus is tender, about 8-10 minutes. In a blender or food processor, puree the asparagus, a third at a time; set aside.

In a Dutch oven or soup kettle, melt butter; stir in flour, salt and pepper. Cook and stir for 2 minutes or until golden. Gradually add cream. Stir in the pureed asparagus and lemon juice; heat through. Garnish with cheese if desired. **Yield:** 8 servings (about 2 quarts).

Asparagus Vinaigrette

(Pictured above)

I love to cook and especially enjoy trying out new recipes. I took a cooking class a number of years ago and discovered this delightful vegetable salad. It's nice for a spring luncheon with the fresh taste of the asparagus,
parsley and chives drizzled with a zesty dressing.
—Marcy Fechtig, Burnt Prairie, Illinois

1-1/2 cups olive oil
1/2 cup white wine vinegar
2 teaspoons Dijon mustard
1/2 teaspoon salt
1/8 teaspoon pepper
3 to 4 radishes, sliced
1/4 cup chopped green pepper
3 tablespoon dill pickle relish
1 tablespoon chopped fresh parsley
1 tablespoon snipped fresh chives
2 pounds fresh asparagus, cooked and drained
Lettuce leaves
3 hard-cooked eggs, sliced
2 medium tomatoes, cut into wedges

In a bowl, whisk together the first five ingredients. Add radishes, green pepper, relish, parsley and chives. Place asparagus in a glass dish; pour dressing over top. Cover and chill at least 4 hours.

To serve, arrange the lettuce on a serving platter; remove asparagus from dressing with a slotted spoon and arrange over lettuce. Garnish with eggs and tomatoes. Drizzle with some of the dressing. **Yield:** 6-8 servings.

Sunny Asparagus Tart

aside; cut remaining pieces in half. Cook all of the asparagus in a small amount of water until crisp-tender, about 3-4 minutes; drain. In a mixing bowl, combine the cream cheese and egg yolk; gradually add cream (mixture will be slightly lumpy). Beat in eggs, one at a time. Add salt and pepper.

Place ham and asparagus pieces (not tips) over crust; pour half of the cream cheese mixture over the top. Bake at 425° for 15 minutes. Pour remaining cream cheese mixture over top. Arrange asparagus tips on top of tart; sprinkle with cheese. Bake at 375° for 40 minutes or until a knife inserted near the center comes out clean. Let stand for 15 minutes before cutting. **Yield:** 6-8 servings.

Sunny Asparagus Tart

(Pictured above)

This tart looks as good as it tastes. The distinctive caraway crust and rich, custard-like filling dotted with tender slices of asparagus make it a dish you'll be proud to serve time after time. —Susan Kuklinski
Delafield, Wisconsin

1-1/2 cups all-purpose flour
1/2 teaspoon caraway seeds
1/8 teaspoon salt
5 tablespoons cold butter
2 tablespoons cold shortening
3 to 5 tablespoons cold water
FILLING:
1-1/2 pounds fresh asparagus
1 package (3 ounces) cream cheese, softened
1 egg yolk
1 cup heavy whipping cream
3 eggs
3/4 teaspoon salt
1/4 teaspoon white pepper
1/4 pound thinly sliced fully cooked ham, julienned
1/3 cup grated Parmesan cheese

In a bowl, combine flour, caraway and salt; cut in butter and shortening until mixture resembles coarse crumbs. Sprinkle with water, 1 tablespoon at a time; stir with a fork until dough forms a ball. On a floured surface, roll dough to fit a 10-in. tart pan. Place dough in pan. Freeze 10 minutes.

Cut the asparagus into 2-1/2-in. pieces. Set tips

Cheesy Asparagus Bites

When I managed a cafeteria, I would cook up different snacks for the staff. These tiny squares with a big asparagus flavor never lasted long. —Lois McAtee
Oceanside, California

1/2 cup diced onion
1 garlic clove, minced
2 tablespoons vegetable oil
2 cups (8 ounces) shredded sharp cheddar cheese
1/4 cup dry bread crumbs
2 tablespoons minced fresh parsley
1/4 teaspoon salt
1/4 teaspoon pepper
1/8 to 1/4 teaspoon dried oregano
1/8 teaspoon hot pepper sauce
4 eggs, beaten
1 pound fresh asparagus, trimmed and cut into 1/2-inch pieces

In a skillet, saute onion and garlic in oil until tender. Combine the cheese, bread crumbs, parsley, salt, pepper, oregano and hot pepper sauce. Stir in the onion mixture and eggs. Cook asparagus in a small amount of water until crisp-tender, about 3-4 minutes; drain well. Stir into cheese mixture.

Pour into a greased 9-in. square baking pan. Bake at 350° for 30 minutes or until a knife inserted near the center comes out clean. Let stand for 15 minutes. Cut into small squares; serve warm. **Yield:** 5 dozen.

Asparagus Roll-Ups

These roll-ups are simply divine. A friend shared the recipe after serving them at a church brunch, where they disappeared quickly. They make a unique finger food, a side dish at supper or a lunch served with soup.
—Clara Nenstiel, Pampa, Texas

16 fresh asparagus spears
16 slices sandwich bread, crusts removed
 1 package (8 ounces) cream cheese,
   softened
 8 bacon strips, cooked and crumbled
 2 tablespoons minced fresh *or* dried
   chives
 1/4 cup butter, melted
 3 tablespoons grated Parmesan cheese

Place asparagus in a skillet with a small amount of water; cook until crisp-tender, about 6-8 minutes. Drain and set aside.

Flatten bread with a rolling pin. Combine the cream cheese, bacon and chives; spread 1 tablespoonful on each slice of bread. Top with an asparagus spear. Roll up tightly; place seam side down on a greased baking sheet. Brush with butter and sprinkle with Parmesan cheese. Cut roll-ups in half. Bake at 400° for 10-12 minutes or until lightly browned. **Yield:** 32 appetizers.

Gingered Pork and Asparagus

My husband and I really enjoy fresh asparagus. So we were thrilled when I found this recipe for asparagus and juicy pork slices smothered in a snappy ginger sauce. —Kathleen Purvis, Franklin, Tennessee

 6 tablespoons apple juice
 6 tablespoons soy sauce
 4 garlic cloves, minced
 1 tablespoon ground ginger
 1 pound pork tenderloin, thinly sliced
 2 tablespoons vegetable oil, *divided*
 1 pound fresh asparagus, cut into 1-inch
   pieces
1-1/2 teaspoons cornstarch
Hot cooked rice, optional

In a large resealable plastic bag or shallow glass container, combine the first four ingredients. Remove 1/3 cup and set aside. Add pork to remaining marinade; seal bag or cover container and turn to coat. Refrigerate for 1 hour.

In a large skillet or wok over medium-high heat, stir-fry half of the pork in 1 tablespoon oil for 2-3 minutes or until no longer pink. Remove pork with a slotted spoon; set aside. Repeat with remaining pork and oil.

In the same skillet, stir-fry the asparagus for 2-3 minutes or until crisp-tender. Stir cornstarch into reserved marinade; add to the skillet. Bring to a boil; cook and stir for 2 minutes or until thickened. Return pork to skillet and heat through. Serve over rice if desired. **Yield:** 4 servings.

Asparagus Bacon Quiche

(Pictured below)

Lovely asparagus peeks out of every slice of this hearty quiche, which is delicious and a little different. I like to make it for special occasions—it's a welcome addition to any brunch buffet. —Suzanne McKinley
Lyons, Georgia

 1 unbaked pastry shell (9 inches)
 1 pound fresh asparagus, trimmed and
   cut into 1-inch pieces
 6 bacon strips, cooked and crumbled
 3 eggs
1-1/2 cups half-and-half cream
 1 cup grated Parmesan cheese, *divided*
 1 tablespoon sliced green onions
 1 teaspoon sugar
 1/2 teaspoon salt
 1/4 teaspoon pepper
Pinch ground nutmeg

Line the unpricked pastry shell with a double thickness of heavy-duty foil. Bake at 450° for 5 minutes; remove foil. Bake 5 minutes more; remove from the oven and set aside.

Cook asparagus in a small amount of water until crisp-tender, about 3-4 minutes; drain well. Arrange the bacon and asparagus in the crust. In a bowl, beat eggs; add cream, 1/2 cup cheese, onions, sugar, salt, pepper and nutmeg. Pour over asparagus. Sprinkle with remaining cheese.

Bake at 400° for 10 minutes. Reduce heat to 350°; bake 23-25 minutes longer or until a knife inserted near the center comes out clean. Let stand for 15 minutes before cutting. **Yield:** 6-8 servings.

Asparagus Bacon Quiche

Rhubarb-Filled Cookies
Rhubarb Chutney
Creamy Rhubarb Crepes

Chapter 2
Rhubarb

Rhubarb Chutney

(Pictured at left)

It's always fun to serve a meat or poultry dish with a twist. This tangy-sweet chutney is a wonderfully different garnish. With fine chunks of rhubarb and raisins, it has a wonderful consistency. It's among our favorite condiments. —Jan Paterson
Anchorage, Alaska

    3/4 cup sugar
    1/3 cup cider vinegar
      1 tablespoon minced garlic
      1 teaspoon ground cumin
      1 tablespoon minced fresh gingerroot
    1/2 teaspoon ground cinnamon
    1/4 to 1/2 teaspoon ground cloves
    1/4 teaspoon crushed red pepper flakes
      4 cups coarsely chopped fresh *or* frozen
        rhubarb, thawed
    1/2 cup chopped red onion
    1/3 cup golden raisins
      1 teaspoon red food coloring, optional

In a large saucepan, combine the first eight ingredients. Bring to a boil. Reduce heat; simmer, uncovered, for 2 minutes or until sugar is dissolved.

Add the rhubarb, onion and raisins. Cook and stir over medium heat for 5-10 minutes or until rhubarb is tender and mixture is slightly thickened. Stir in food coloring if desired. Cool completely. Store in the refrigerator. **Yield:** about 3 cups.

Rhubarb-Filled Cookies

(Pictured at left)

I won a blue ribbon at our local fair for these tender cookies. They're so pretty with the filling peeking through the dough. When not just any cookie will do, try making these and watch the smiles appear.
—Pauline Bondy, Grand Forks, North Dakota

      1 cup butter, softened
      1 cup sugar
      1 cup packed brown sugar
      4 eggs
    4-1/2 cups all-purpose flour
      1 teaspoon baking soda
      1 teaspoon salt
FILLING:
    3-1/2 cups chopped fresh *or* frozen rhubarb,
        thawed
    1-1/2 cups sugar
      6 tablespoons water, *divided*
    1/4 cup cornstarch
      1 teaspoon vanilla extract

In a mixing bowl, cream butter and sugars. Add eggs, one at a time, beating well after each addition. Combine the flour, baking soda and salt; gradually add to creamed mixture and mix well (dough will be sticky).

For filling, combine the rhubarb, sugar and 2 tablespoons water in a large saucepan. Bring to a boil. Reduce heat; simmer, uncovered, for 10 minutes or until thickened, stirring frequently. Combine cornstarch and remaining water until smooth; stir into rhubarb mixture. Bring to a boil; cook and stir for 2 minutes or until thickened. Remove from the heat; stir in vanilla.

Drop dough by tablespoonfuls 2 in. apart onto ungreased baking sheets. Using the end of a wooden spoon handle, make an indentation in the center of each cookie; fill with a rounded teaspoon of filling. Top with 1/2 teaspoon of dough, allowing some filling to show. Bake at 375° for 8-10 minutes or until lightly browned. **Yield:** about 4-1/2 dozen.

Editor's Note: Any leftover rhubarb filling may be stored, covered, in the refrigerator and used as a spread on toast or a topping for ice cream.

Rhubarb Reference

Tender, young stalks are easiest to use. They only need to be cut before cooking. Rhubarb with tougher stalks can be peeled with a vegetable peeler to remove fibrous strings before they are cut or cooked.
—Marie Mertz, Racine, Wisconsin

Creamy Rhubarb Crepes

(Pictured on page 10)

Fixing rhubarb this way brings a spring "zing" to the table. I adapted this crepe recipe, which originally featured strawberry jelly, from one I loved as a child.
—Stasha Wampler, Gate City, Virginia

> **3 eggs**
> **1 cup milk**
> **5 tablespoons butter, melted**
> **1/4 cup sugar**
> **1/4 teaspoon salt**
> **1 cup all-purpose flour**
> **Additional butter**
> **SAUCE/FILLING:**
> **1 cup sugar**
> **1 tablespoon cornstarch**
> **1/4 teaspoon ground cinnamon**
> **2 cups thinly sliced fresh *or* frozen rhubarb, thawed**
> **1 package (8 ounces) cream cheese, softened**
> **Confectioners' sugar**

In a bowl, whisk eggs, milk, melted butter, sugar and salt. Beat in flour until smooth; let stand for 30 minutes. Melt 1/2 teaspoon butter in an 8-in. non-stick skillet. Pour 1/4 cup batter into the center of skillet; lift and turn pan to cover bottom. Cook until lightly browned; turn and brown the other side. Remove to a wire rack; cover with paper towel. Repeat with remaining batter, adding butter to skillet as needed.

Meanwhile, for sauce, combine the sugar, cornstarch and cinnamon in a saucepan. Stir in rhubarb. Bring to a boil over medium heat; cook and stir for 2 minutes or until slightly thickened and rhubarb is tender. Remove from the heat; cool slightly.

For filling, in a mixing bowl, beat cream cheese and 1/4 cup of the rhubarb sauce until smooth and creamy. Place a rounded tablespoonful on each crepe; fold in half and in half again, forming a triangle. Dust with confectioners' sugar. Serve with remaining sauce. **Yield:** 10 crepes.

Rhubarb Crumble

When I met my English husband and served him just the crumble, he said it was fantastic but really needed a custard sauce over it. We found a terrific sauce recipe from England, and now the pair is perfect together.
—Amy Freeman, Cave Creek, Arizona

> **8 cups chopped fresh *or* frozen rhubarb**
> **1-1/4 cups sugar, *divided***
> **2-1/2 cups all-purpose flour**
> **1/4 cup packed brown sugar**
> **1/4 cup quick-cooking oats**
> **1 cup cold butter**
> **CUSTARD SAUCE:**
> **6 egg yolks**
> **1/2 cup sugar**
> **2 cups heavy whipping cream**
> **1-1/4 teaspoons vanilla extract**

In a saucepan, combine rhubarb and 3/4 cup of sugar. Cover and cook over medium heat, stirring occasionally, until the rhubarb is tender, about 10 minutes. Pour into a greased 13-in. x 9-in. x 2-in. baking dish. In a bowl, combine flour, brown sugar, oats and remaining sugar. Cut in butter until crumbly; sprinkle over rhubarb. Bake at 400° for 30 minutes.

Meanwhile, in a saucepan, whisk the egg yolks and sugar; stir in cream. Cook and stir over low heat until a thermometer reads 160° and mixture thickens, about 15-20 minutes. Remove from the heat; stir in vanilla. Serve warm over rhubarb crumble. **Yield:** 12 servings (2-1/2 cups sauce).

Rhubarb Cheesecake Dessert

Rhubarb Cheesecake Dessert

(Pictured at left)

After moving to our home over 20 years ago, we were thrilled to discover a huge rhubarb patch. Each spring, my family looks forward to these sensational squares.
—Joyce Krumwiede, Mankato, Minnesota

> **1 cup all-purpose flour**
> **1/2 cup packed brown sugar**
> **1/4 teaspoon salt**
> **1/4 cup cold butter**
> **1/2 cup chopped walnuts**
> **1 teaspoon vanilla extract**

FILLING:
  - 2 packages (8 ounces *each*) cream cheese, softened
  - 3/4 cup sugar
  - 3 eggs
  - 1 teaspoon vanilla extract

TOPPING:
  - 3 cups chopped fresh *or* frozen rhubarb, thawed and drained
  - 1 cup sugar
  - 1/4 cup water
  - 1 tablespoon cornstarch
  - 1/4 teaspoon ground cinnamon
  - 3 to 4 drops red food coloring, optional

In a bowl, combine flour, brown sugar and salt; cut in butter until mixture resembles coarse crumbs. Stir in walnuts and vanilla. Press into a greased 13-in. x 9-in. x 2-in. baking dish. Bake at 375° for 10 minutes. Cool slightly.

In a mixing bowl, beat cream cheese and sugar until light and fluffy. Add eggs and vanilla; mix well. Pour over the crust. Bake for 20-25 minutes or until center is set and edges are light brown. Cool.

In a saucepan, combine the rhubarb, sugar, water, cornstarch and cinnamon; bring to a boil over medium heat. Cook, stirring constantly, until mixture thickens, about 5 minutes. Stir in food coloring if desired. Remove from the heat; cool. Pour over filling. Cover and refrigerate for at least 1 hour. **Yield:** 12-15 servings.

Spinach Salad with Rhubarb Dressing

Spinach salad is excellent with this tangy topping. The rhubarb adds rosy color. —Twila Mitchell
Lindsburg, Kansas

  - 2 cups chopped fresh *or* frozen rhubarb
  - 1/2 cup sugar
  - 1/4 cup vinegar
  - 3/4 cup vegetable oil
  - 3 tablespoons grated onion
  - 1-1/2 teaspoons Worcestershire sauce
  - 1/2 teaspoon salt

SALAD:
  - 6 cups torn fresh spinach
  - 6 bacon strips, cooked and crumbled
  - 1/2 cup fresh bean sprouts
  - 1/2 cup shredded cheddar cheese
  - 1 to 2 hard-cooked eggs, chopped

In a saucepan, combine rhubarb, sugar and vinegar; cook over medium heat until tender, about 6

Perfect Rhubarb Pie

minutes. Drain, reserving 6 tablespoons juice; discard pulp. Pour juice into a jar with tight-fitting lid; add oil, onion, Worcestershire sauce and salt. Shake well. Refrigerate for 1 hour. Just before serving, combine salad ingredients in a large bowl. Add dressing; toss to coat. **Yield:** 6-8 servings.

Perfect Rhubarb Pie

(Pictured above)

Nothing hides the tangy rhubarb in this lovely pie, which has just the right balance of sweet and tart. Serving it is a nice way to celebrate the end of winter!
—Ellen Benninger, Stoneboro, Pennsylvania

  - 4 cups sliced fresh rhubarb
  - 4 cups boiling water
  - 1-1/2 cups sugar
  - 3 tablespoons all-purpose flour
  - 1 teaspoon quick-cooking tapioca
  - 1 egg
  - 2 teaspoons cold water
  - Pastry for double-crust pie (9 inches)
  - 1 tablespoon butter

Place rhubarb in a colander and pour water over it; set aside. In a bowl, combine sugar, flour and tapioca; mix well. Add drained rhubarb; toss to coat. Let stand for 15 minutes. Beat egg and water; add to rhubarb mixture and mix well.

Line a 9-in. pie plate with bottom pastry. Add filling. Dot with butter. Cover with remaining pastry; flute edges. Cut slits in top crust. Bake at 400° for 15 minutes. Reduce heat to 350°; bake 40-50 minutes longer or until crust is golden brown and filling is bubbly. **Yield:** 8 servings.

Rhubarb Slush

Rhubarb Slush

(Pictured above)

This thirst-quenching slush is a fun way to use rhubarb. I serve it for special get-togethers. The rosy color and tangy flavor of this spring crop come through in every sip. —Theresa Pearson, Ogilvie, Minnesota

3 cups chopped fresh *or* frozen rhubarb
1 cup water
1/3 cup sugar
1 cup apple juice
1 can (6 ounces) frozen pink lemonade concentrate, thawed
1 bottle (2 liters) lemon-lime soda

In a saucepan, combine rhubarb, water and sugar; bring to a boil. Reduce heat; cover and simmer for 5 minutes or until rhubarb is tender. Cool for about 30 minutes. In a food processor or blender, puree mixture, half at a time. Stir in apple juice and lemonade. Pour into a freezer container; cover and freeze until firm. Let stand at room temperature for 45 minutes before serving.

For individual servings, scoop 1/3 cup into a glass and fill with soda. To serve a group, place all of mixture in a large pitcher or punch bowl; add soda and stir. Serve immediately. **Yield:** about 10 servings.

Rhubarb Bread Pudding

This old-fashioned pudding is a great way to use up day-old bread. Nothing enhances this traditional dessert better than garden-grown rhubarb.
—Virginia Andersen, Palermo, North Dakota

8 slices bread, lightly toasted
1-1/2 cups milk
1/4 cup butter
5 eggs, lightly beaten
3 cups chopped fresh *or* frozen rhubarb, thawed
1-1/2 cups sugar
1/2 teaspoon ground cinnamon
1/4 teaspoon salt
1/2 cup packed brown sugar

Remove crusts from bread; cut into 1/2-in. cubes. Place in a greased 1-1/2-qt. baking dish. In a saucepan, heat milk over medium heat until bubbles form around sides of pan; remove from the heat. Stir in butter until melted. Pour over bread; let stand for 15 minutes.

In a bowl, combine the eggs, rhubarb, sugar, cinnamon and salt; stir into bread mixture. Sprinkle with brown sugar. Bake at 350° for 45-50 minutes or until set. Serve warm. Refrigerate leftovers. **Yield:** 8 servings.

Peachy Rhubarb Pie

We have an abundance of "pieplant" in our garden, so I save every rhubarb recipe I come across. My husband especially loves the combination of rhubarb and peaches in this pie. —Phyllis Galloway
Roswell, Georgia

  1 can (8-1/2 ounces) sliced peaches
  2 cups chopped fresh *or* frozen rhubarb,
    thawed and drained
  1 cup sugar
  1/4 cup flaked coconut
  3 tablespoons quick-cooking tapioca
  1 teaspoon vanilla extract
Pastry for double-crust pie (9 inches)
  1 tablespoon butter

Drain peaches, reserving syrup; chop the peaches. Place peaches and syrup in a bowl; add rhubarb, sugar, coconut, tapioca and vanilla. Line a 9-in. pie plate with the bottom pastry.

  Add filling; dot with butter. Top with remaining pastry or a lattice crust; flute edges. If using a full top crust, cut slits in it. Bake at 350° for 1 hour or until crust is golden brown and filling is bubbly. **Yield:** 6-8 servings.

Rhubarb Granola Crisp

When my husband and I moved to our house in town, the rhubarb patch had to come along! This is a hit whether I serve it warm with ice cream or cold.
—Arlene Beitz, Cambridge, Ontario

  4 cups chopped fresh *or* frozen rhubarb,
    thawed and drained
1-1/4 cups all-purpose flour, *divided*
  1/4 cup sugar
  1/2 cup strawberry jam
1-1/2 cups granola cereal
  1/2 cup packed brown sugar
  1/2 cup chopped pecans
  1/2 teaspoon ground cinnamon
  1/2 teaspoon ground ginger
  1/2 cup cold butter
Ice cream, optional

In a bowl, combine the rhubarb, 1/4 cup flour and sugar; stir in jam and set aside. In another bowl, combine the granola, brown sugar, pecans, cinnamon, ginger and remaining flour. Cut in butter until the mixture resembles coarse crumbs.

  Press 2 cups of the granola mixture into a greased 8-in. square baking dish; spread rhubarb mixture over the crust. Sprinkle with remaining

granola mixture. Bake at 375° for 30-40 minutes or until filling is bubbly and topping is golden brown. Serve warm with ice cream if desired. **Yield:** 9 servings.

Strawberry Rhubarb Sauce

(Pictured below)

This versatile sauce brings a sunny new taste to pound cake, ice cream and bread pudding. I wouldn't be without it! —Mary Pittman, Shawnee, Kansas

2-1/2 cups chopped fresh *or* frozen rhubarb
  1 cup water
  1/2 cup sugar
  2 tablespoons grated lemon peel
  1/4 teaspoon salt
  1 cup sliced fresh *or* frozen unsweetened
    strawberries
  2 tablespoons lemon juice
  1/4 teaspoon ground cinnamon
  3 to 4 drops red food coloring, optional
Pound *or* angel food cake

In a saucepan, combine rhubarb, water, sugar, lemon peel and salt; bring to a boil. Reduce heat. Cook, uncovered, over medium heat until rhubarb is soft, about 10-15 minutes.

  Remove from the heat and let stand for 5 minutes. Stir in strawberries, lemon juice and cinnamon. Add food coloring if desired. Cool. Serve over cake. **Yield:** 3 cups.

Strawberry Rhubarb Sauce

Rhubarb Custard Cake

(Pictured below)

Rhubarb thrives in my northern garden and is one of the few crops the pesky moose don't bother! Of all the rhubarb desserts I've tried, this pudding cake is my top choice. It has old-fashioned appeal but is so simple to prepare. —Evelyn Gebhardt, Kasilof, Alaska

    1 package (18-1/4 ounces) yellow cake mix
    4 cups chopped fresh *or* frozen rhubarb
    1 cup sugar
    1 cup heavy whipping cream
Whipped cream and fresh mint, optional

Prepare cake batter according to package directions. Pour into a greased 13-in. x 9-in. x 2-in. baking dish. Sprinkle with rhubarb and sugar. Slowly pour cream over top.

Bake at 350° for 40-45 minutes or until golden brown. Cool for 15 minutes before serving. Garnish with whipped cream and mint if desired. Refrigerate leftovers. **Yield:** 12-15 servings.

Rosy Rhubarb Mold

Any meal benefits from this ruby-colored salad—it's always a refreshing accompaniment. I never have leftovers, since the combination of sweet, tangy and crunchy ingredients is so irresistible.

—Regina Albright, Southhaven, Mississippi

Rhubarb Custard Cake

 Uses less fat, sugar or salt. Includes Nutritional Analysis and Diabetic Exchanges.

    4 cups chopped fresh *or* frozen rhubarb
    1 cup water
  2/3 cup sugar
  1/4 teaspoon salt
    1 package (6 ounces) strawberry gelatin
1-1/2 cups cold water
  1/4 cup lemon juice
    2 cans (11 ounces *each*) mandarin
        oranges, drained
    1 cup chopped celery
Optional garnishes: lettuce leaves, sliced
    strawberries, green grapes, sour cream and
    ground nutmeg

In a saucepan, combine the rhubarb, water, sugar and salt; bring to a boil over medium heat. Boil for 1-2 minutes or until the rhubarb is tender; remove from the heat. Stir in the gelatin until dissolved. Stir in the cold water and lemon juice. Chill until partially set.

Fold in oranges and celery. Pour into a 6-cup mold or an 8-in. square dish that has been coated with nonstick cooking spray. Chill until set. Unmold onto lettuce leaves or cut into squares. If desired, garnish with fruit and serve with sour cream sprinkled with nutmeg. **Yield:** 12 servings.

Nutritional Analysis: One 1/2-cup serving (prepared with sugar-free gelatin; calculated without garnishes) equals 79 calories, 98 mg sodium, 0 cholesterol, 19 g carbohydrate, 2 g protein, trace fat. **Diabetic Exchange:** 1 fruit.

Rhubarb Streusel Muffins

What a pleasure it is to set out a basket of these rhubarb muffins…although the basket doesn't stay full for very long! I have six children and two grandsons, so I do a lot of baking. The snacks are based on a coffee cake recipe. —Sandra Moreside, Regina, Saskatchewan

  1/2 cup butter, softened
    1 cup packed brown sugar
  1/2 cup sugar
    1 egg
    2 cups all-purpose flour
    1 teaspoon baking powder
  1/2 teaspoon baking soda
  1/8 teaspoon salt
    1 cup (8 ounces) sour cream
    3 cups chopped fresh *or* frozen rhubarb,
        thawed
TOPPING:
  1/2 cup chopped pecans

1/4 cup packed brown sugar
1 teaspoon ground cinnamon
1 tablespoon cold butter

In a mixing bowl, cream the butter and sugars. Add egg; beat well. Combine the flour, baking powder, baking soda and salt; add to creamed mixture alternately with the sour cream. Fold in the rhubarb. Fill paper-lined or greased muffin cups three-fourths full.

For topping, combine the pecans, brown sugar and cinnamon in a small bowl; cut in butter until crumbly. Sprinkle over the batter. Bake at 350° for 22-25 minutes or until a toothpick inserted near the center comes out clean. Cool for 5 minutes before removing from pans to wire racks. **Yield:** about 1-1/2 dozen.

Rhubarb Jelly-Roll Cake

This jelly-roll recipe came from my mom's cookbook, circa 1940. It's continued to be a family classic and is popular at church potlucks. The kids in my 4-H cooking class have fun making it, too. —Donna Stratton
Carson City, Nevada

6 cups chopped fresh *or* frozen rhubarb, thawed
2-3/4 cups sugar, *divided*
2 teaspoons ground cinnamon
1/4 teaspoon ground allspice
1/8 teaspoon ground cloves
4 eggs
1 teaspoon lemon extract
3/4 cup all-purpose flour
1 teaspoon baking powder
1/2 teaspoon salt
Confectioners' sugar

In a saucepan, combine the rhubarb, 2 cups sugar, cinnamon, allspice and cloves. Bring to a boil. Reduce heat; cook, uncovered, over medium heat until thickened. Cool completely.

In a mixing bowl, beat eggs on high speed until thick and lemon-colored. Gradually add remaining sugar, beating until thick and light-colored. Beat in extract. Combine the flour, baking powder and salt; gradually add to egg mixture.

Grease a 15-in. x 10-in. x 1-in. baking pan and line with waxed paper; grease and flour the paper. Spread batter into pan. Bake at 375° for 15 minutes or until cake springs back when lightly touched. Cool for 5 minutes. Turn onto a kitchen towel dusted with confectioners' sugar. Peel off waxed paper. Roll up cake in towel jelly-roll style, starting with a short side. Cool.

Carefully unroll cake. Spread filling over cake to within 1 in. of edges. Roll up again. Store in the refrigerator. Dust with confectioners' sugar just before serving. **Yield:** 10-12 servings.

Rhubarb Fritters

Rhubarb Fritters

(Pictured above)

I got this recipe from my niece's son. Since we live in apple country, we have enjoyed eating from-scratch apple fritters for many years. This rhubarb treat is a nice change for spring when apples are few and rhubarb is plentiful. —Helen Budinock
Wolcott, New York

1 cup all-purpose flour
1 cup plus 1 tablespoon sugar, *divided*
1/2 teaspoon salt
2 eggs, *separated*
1/2 cup milk
1 tablespoon butter, melted
2 cups finely chopped fresh *or* frozen rhubarb, thawed and drained
Oil for deep-fat frying
Confectioners' sugar

In a medium bowl, combine flour, 1 cup sugar and salt. In another bowl, whisk egg yolks, milk and butter. Gradually add to the dry ingredients, stirring until smooth. Toss rhubarb with the remaining sugar; gently stir into batter. In a mixing bowl, beat egg whites until stiff. Fold into batter.

In an electric skillet or deep-fat fryer, heat oil to 375°. Drop batter by tablespoonfuls into oil. Fry, a few at a time, turning with a slotted spoon until golden brown. Drain on paper towels. Dust with confectioners' sugar. Serve warm. **Yield:** about 3 dozen.

Grilled Three-Pepper Salad
Bell Pepper Enchiladas
Colorful Apricot Chutney
Red Pepper Soup

Chapter 3
Peppers

Red Pepper Soup

(Pictured at left)

While I don't have scientific proof of it, this soup works for me as a head cold remedy! It is a good gift to take when visiting a sick friend, too. For a pretty touch, top the soup with grated cheese and parsley.
—*Barb Nelson, Victoria, British Columbia*

        6 medium sweet red peppers, chopped
        2 medium carrots, chopped
        2 medium onions, chopped
        1 celery rib, chopped
        4 garlic cloves, minced
        1 tablespoon olive oil
        2 cans (one 49-1/2 ounces, one 14-1/2
            ounces) chicken broth
    1/2 cup uncooked long grain rice
        2 tablespoons minced fresh thyme
            or 2 teaspoons dried thyme
    1-1/2 teaspoons salt
    1/4 teaspoon pepper
    1/8 to 1/4 teaspoon cayenne pepper
    1/8 to 1/4 teaspoon crushed red pepper flakes

In a large Dutch oven or soup kettle, saute red peppers, carrots, onions, celery and garlic in oil until tender. Stir in the broth, rice, thyme, salt, pepper and cayenne; bring to a boil.

Reduce heat; cover and simmer for 20-25 minutes or until the vegetables and rice are tender. Cool for 30 minutes. Puree in small batches in a blender; return to pan. Add red pepper flakes; heat through. **Yield:** 10-12 servings (about 3 quarts).

Colorful Apricot Chutney

(Pictured at left)

You can use this chutney as an appetizer on crackers ...or try mixing it with cream cheese for a spread. When the local Extension office held a "Pepper Day", I entered it in the recipe contest. It ended up winning first prize.   —*Lucile Cline, Wichita, Kansas*

        3 large sweet red peppers, diced
        12 ounces dried apricots, diced
        1 cup raisins
        1 cup sugar
        1 large onion, finely chopped
    3/4 cup red wine vinegar
        5 garlic cloves, minced
    1-1/2 teaspoons salt
    1-1/2 teaspoons crushed red pepper flakes
    1/4 teaspoon ground ginger
    1/4 teaspoon ground cumin
    1/4 teaspoon ground mustard

In a large heavy saucepan, combine all ingredients; bring to a boil. Reduce heat; simmer, uncovered, for 25-30 minutes or until thickened, stirring occasionally. Cover and refrigerate.

Serve as an accompaniment to pork or chicken. Chutney may be stored in the refrigerator for up to 1 month. **Yield:** 4 cups.

Bell Pepper Enchiladas

(Pictured at left)

Peppers are probably the vegetable I use most. My freezer's stocked in case I discover a new recipe or want to whip up an old favorite, like these enchiladas.
—*Melissa Cowser, Greenville, Texas*

        2 medium green peppers, chopped
    1/2 cup shredded cheddar cheese
    1/2 cup shredded Monterey Jack cheese
    1/2 cup diced process cheese (Velveeta)
        4 flour tortillas (8 inches)
        1 small jalapeno pepper, minced, optional
        1 cup salsa, *divided*
    Additional shredded cheese, optional

Sprinkle the green peppers and cheeses down the center of tortillas; add jalapeno if desired. Roll up. Spread 1/2 cup salsa in a shallow baking dish. Place tortillas seam side down over salsa. Top with remaining salsa. Bake at 350° for 20 minutes or until heated through. Sprinkle with additional cheese if desired. **Yield:** 4 enchiladas.

Editor's Note: When cutting or seeding hot peppers, use rubber or plastic gloves to protect your hands. Avoid touching your face.

Peppery Philly Steaks

(Pictured below)

Since we love to cook and eat, my husband and I are always developing new recipes. This is one we especially enjoy when we have fresh peppers. —Edie Fitch
Clifton, Arizona

1-1/2 pounds boneless sirloin steak, cut
    into 1/4-inch strips
1 *each* medium green and sweet red
    peppers, julienned
1 large onion, thinly sliced
3 tablespoons vegetable oil
2 tablespoons butter
5 to 6 French *or* Italian sandwich rolls,
    split
2 cans (4 ounces *each*) whole green
    chilies, drained and halved
5 to 6 slices Swiss cheese

In a large skillet, cook steak, peppers and onion in oil until meat reaches desired doneness and vegetables are soft. Spread butter on rolls; top with meat mixture, chilies and cheese. Wrap in heavy-duty foil. Bake at 350° for 10-12 minutes or until heated through and cheese is melted. **Yield:** 5-6 servings.

Grilled Three-Pepper Salad

(Pictured on page 18)

I have been cooking since my mother taught me how at an early age. I enjoy it, and I'm always trying new recipes. This one's both flavorful and colorful.
—Ruth Wickard, York, Pennsylvania

Peppery Philly Steaks

2 *each* large green, sweet red and yellow
    peppers, cut into 1-inch pieces
1 large red onion, halved and thinly sliced
1 pound bulk mozzarella cheese, cut into
    bite-size cubes
1 can (6 ounces) pitted ripe olives,
    drained and halved
VINAIGRETTE:
  2/3 cup olive oil
  1/3 cup red wine vinegar
  2 tablespoons lemon juice
  2 tablespoons Dijon mustard
  1 tablespoon minced fresh basil *or* 1
    teaspoon dried basil
  1/2 teaspoon cayenne pepper
  1/2 teaspoon garlic powder

Thread peppers onto metal or soaked wooden skewers; grill or broil for 10-12 minutes or until edges are browned. Remove from skewers and place in a large bowl. Add onion, mozzarella and olives; toss gently. Cover and refrigerate.

Combine vinaigrette ingredients in a jar with tight-fitting lid; shake well. Pour over the pepper mixture just before serving; toss to coat. **Yield:** 10-12 servings.

Pepper-Topped Pizza

We prefer this recipe over regular pizza. Its tomato and pepper topping is irresistible. Plus, it can be on the table in less than half an hour! —Sonia Speh
Gordonsville, Virginia

1 tube (12 ounces) refrigerated flaky
    buttermilk biscuits
1 tablespoon olive oil
1/2 cup chopped green pepper
1/2 cup chopped sweet yellow pepper
1/2 cup chopped tomato
1/4 cup chopped onion
1/2 teaspoon garlic powder
1/4 teaspoon dried basil
1/4 teaspoon dried oregano
1/4 cup shredded Parmesan cheese

Split biscuits in half horizontally. Arrange on a lightly greased 12-in. round pizza pan; press dough together to seal the edges. Brush with oil. Sprinkle with peppers, tomato, onion, garlic powder, basil and oregano.

Bake at 400° for 15-20 minutes or until crust is golden brown. Cover edges with foil to prevent over-browning if necessary. Sprinkle with Parmesan cheese. Serve immediately. **Yield:** 4-6 servings.

Chicken-Stuffed Green Peppers

(Pictured above)

Both for a family meal and for entertaining, this is a dish I serve frequently. It's very appealing to the eye.
—Shelley Armstrong, Buffalo Center, Iowa

4 large green peppers
1/3 cup chopped onion
1 garlic clove, minced
2 tablespoons butter
3 cups diced cooked chicken
2 cups chicken broth
1 package (6 ounces) long grain brown
and wild rice blend
1/3 cup sliced celery
1/4 cup finely chopped carrot
1/4 teaspoon dried basil
1/4 teaspoon dried thyme
1 can (14-1/2 ounces) diced tomatoes,
undrained
1 cup chopped fresh mushrooms
1/2 cup chopped zucchini
1/4 cup grated Parmesan cheese

Cut tops off peppers; remove seeds. In a large kettle, cook peppers in boiling water for 3 minutes. Drain and rinse in cold water; set aside.

In a large saucepan, saute onion and garlic in butter until tender. Add chicken, broth, rice with contents of seasoning packet, celery, carrot, basil and thyme; bring to a boil. Reduce heat; cover and simmer for 25 minutes or until the rice is almost tender. Remove from the heat; stir in tomatoes, mushrooms and zucchini.

Spoon rice mixture into the peppers; place in a greased 2-qt. baking dish. Spoon the remaining rice mixture around peppers. Cover and bake at 350° for 25-30 minutes or until the peppers are tender and filling is heated through. Uncover and sprinkle with Parmesan cheese; bake 5 minutes longer. **Yield:** 4 servings.

Pepper Avocado Salsa

Pepper Avocado Salsa

(Pictured above)

Much of our summer menu is done on the grill, and peppers and avocados are favorites in my family. That led me to create this recipe to help spice up our barbecued entrees. I have also served it as an appetizer on thin wedges of bread and as a topping for easy country-style dishes like chicken and rice pilaf.
—Theresa Mullens, Gill, Massachusetts

   2 medium tomatoes, diced
1/4 cup *each* diced green, sweet red and
      yellow pepper
1/4 cup diced red onion
   2 tablespoons olive oil
   2 tablespoons lime juice
   1 tablespoon white wine vinegar
   1 garlic clove, minced
   1 tablespoon minced fresh basil *or* 1
      teaspoon dried basil
   1 tablespoon minced fresh dill *or* 1
      teaspoon dill weed
   1 teaspoon sugar
3/4 teaspoon minced fresh thyme *or* 1/4
      teaspoon dried thyme
Dash hot pepper sauce
   1 large ripe avocado

In a bowl, combine the first 12 ingredients. Cover and refrigerate. Just before serving, peel and chop the avocado; stir into the salsa. Serve with chips or as an accompaniment to meat, poultry or fish. **Yield:** 3-1/2 cups.

Honey Pork and Peppers

I'm always trying new recipes on my husband and son. This easy, quick and delicious one is a keeper—a nice change from pork roast or pork chops. —Carol Heim
Nokesville, Virginia

1-1/2 pounds boneless pork, cut into 1-inch
      cubes
   2 tablespoons vegetable oil
   1 envelope brown gravy mix
   1 cup water
1/4 cup honey
   3 tablespoons soy sauce
   2 tablespoons red wine vinegar
1/2 teaspoon ground ginger
1/8 teaspoon garlic powder
   1 medium onion, cut into wedges
   1 medium sweet red pepper, cut
      into 1-inch pieces
   1 medium green pepper, cut into 1-inch
      pieces
Hot cooked rice

In a large skillet over medium heat, cook pork in oil until browned, about 15 minutes. Combine gravy mix, water, honey, soy sauce, vinegar, ginger and garlic powder; add to the pork. Cover and simmer for 20 minutes, stirring occasionally. Add onion and peppers; cook 5-10 minutes longer. Serve over rice. **Yield:** 4-6 servings.

Pepperoni Pizza Dip

Similar to a pizza with a creamy crust, this spicy dip dotted with chopped peppers is absolutely delicious. I love to incorporate bell peppers into my cooking because of the color and distinctive flavor they impart.
—Connie Bryant, Wallingford, Kentucky

   1 package (8 ounces) cream cheese,
      softened
1/2 cup sour cream
1/8 teaspoon dried oregano
1/8 teaspoon garlic powder
1/8 teaspoon cayenne pepper
1/2 cup pizza sauce
3/4 cup chopped green pepper
  10 pepperoni slices, quartered
1/4 cup sliced green onions
1/2 cup shredded mozzarella cheese
Toasted bread rounds *or* breadsticks

In a mixing bowl, combine the first five ingredients. Spread into an ungreased 9-in. pie plate or serving plate. Cover with pizza sauce; top with green pepper, pepperoni and onions. Bake at 350° for 10 minutes. Sprinkle with cheese. Bake 5-8 minutes longer or until cheese is melted. Serve with bread rounds or breadsticks. **Yield:** 8-10 servings.

Green Pepper Saute

This zippy dish with tender pepper strips is simple to make, popular at potlucks and a great companion for any meat entree. —Joyce Turley, Slaughters, Kentucky

    3 large green peppers, cut into 1/2-inch
       strips
    1 cup sliced celery
    1 small onion, thinly sliced
    1 garlic clove, minced
    2 tablespoons vegetable oil
    1 can (15 ounces) tomato sauce
  1/2 teaspoon dried basil
Salt and pepper to taste
  1/2 cup crushed seasoned salad croutons

In a large skillet, saute the peppers, celery, onion and garlic in oil until tender. Stir in the tomato sauce, basil, salt and pepper. Simmer, uncovered, for 8-10 minutes or until vegetables are tender and mixture is thickened. Sprinkle with croutons. **Yield:** 4 servings.

Pepper Steak

I sometimes like to add mushrooms and water chestnuts to this savory steak as well.   —Cindy Gerber Ayr, Ontario

1-1/4 cups beef broth, *divided*
  1/4 cup soy sauce
1-1/4 teaspoons ground ginger
  1/2 teaspoon sugar
  1/4 teaspoon pepper
1-1/2 pounds boneless round steak, cut into
       strips
    1 garlic clove, minced
  1/4 cup olive oil
    4 medium green peppers, julienned
    2 large tomatoes, peeled and chopped
    3 tablespoons cornstarch
Hot cooked rice

In a small bowl, combine 3/4 cup broth, soy sauce, ginger, sugar and pepper; set aside. In a skillet or wok over medium-high heat, brown beef and garlic in oil. Add peppers and tomatoes. Cook and stir until peppers are crisp-tender, about 3 minutes.

Stir soy sauce mixture and add to pan. Cover and cook until the meat is tender, about 15 minutes. Combine cornstarch with the remaining broth until smooth; add to pan. Bring to a boil; cook and stir for 2 minutes. Serve over rice. **Yield:** 8 servings.

Pickled Peppers

(Pictured below)

Well received at potlucks, this colorful and tasty dish adds zest to the menu. I also make it as a salad or accompaniment for a luncheon or dinner at home.
                    —Heather Prendergast, Sundre, Alberta

    2 *each* medium green, sweet red and
       yellow peppers, cut into 1-inch pieces
    1 large red onion, halved and thinly sliced
    1 cup cider vinegar
    1 cup sugar
  1/3 cup water
    2 teaspoons mixed pickling spices
  1/2 teaspoon celery seed

In a large glass bowl, combine the peppers and onion; set aside. In a saucepan, combine the vinegar, sugar and water. Place the pickling spices and celery seed in a double thickness of cheesecloth; bring up the corners of the cloth and tie with string to form a bag.

Add to saucepan. Bring to a boil; boil for 1 minute. Transfer spice bag to pepper mixture. Pour the vinegar mixture over all. Cover and refrigerate for 24 hours, stirring occasionally. Discard spice bag. Peppers may be stored in the refrigerator for up to 1 month. **Yield:** 4 cups.

Pickled Peppers

Green Bean Mushroom Pie
German-Style Green Beans

Chapter 4
Beans

German-Style Green Beans

(Pictured at left)

My mother-in-law introduced me to this quick down-home dish about 50 years ago when I was a new bride. The tender green beans are topped with diced bacon and a classic sweet-sour glaze. Guests always ask for the recipe.—Vivian Steers, Central Islip, New York

> 1 pound fresh green beans, cut into 2-inch pieces
> 3 bacon strips, diced
> 1 medium onion, quartered and sliced
> 2 teaspoons cornstarch
> 1/4 teaspoon salt
> 1/4 teaspoon ground mustard
> 1/2 cup water
> 1 tablespoon brown sugar
> 1 tablespoon cider vinegar

Place beans in a saucepan and cover with water; bring to a boil. Cook, uncovered, for 8-10 minutes or until crisp-tender; drain and set aside. In a skillet, cook bacon over medium heat until crisp. Remove to paper towels. Drain, reserving 1 tablespoon drippings. In the same skillet, saute onion in drippings until tender.

In a bowl, combine cornstarch, salt, mustard and water until smooth. Stir into onion. Bring to a boil; cook and stir for 1-2 minutes or until thickened. Stir in sugar and vinegar. Add beans; heat through. Sprinkle with bacon. **Yield:** 3-4 servings.

Green Bean Mushroom Pie

(Pictured at left)

Fresh green bean flavor stands out in this pretty lattice-topped pie. A flaky golden crust holds the savory bean, mushroom and cream cheese filling.
—Tara Walworth, Maple Park, Illinois

> 3 cups sliced fresh mushrooms
> 4 tablespoons butter, *divided*
> 2-1/2 cups chopped onions
> 6 cups cut fresh green beans (1-inch pieces)
> 2 teaspoons minced fresh thyme *or* 3/4 teaspoon dried thyme
> 1/2 teaspoon salt
> 1/4 teaspoon pepper
> 1 package (8 ounces) cream cheese, cubed
> 1/2 cup milk
> CRUST:
> 2-1/2 cups all-purpose flour
> 2 teaspoons baking powder
> 1 teaspoon dill weed
> 1/4 teaspoon salt
> 1 cup cold butter
> 1 cup (8 ounces) sour cream
> 1 egg
> 1 tablespoon heavy whipping cream

In a large skillet, saute the mushrooms in 1 tablespoon butter until tender; drain and set aside. In the same skillet, saute the onions and beans in remaining butter for 18-20 minutes or until the beans are crisp-tender. Add the thyme, salt, pepper, cream cheese, milk and mushrooms. Cook and stir until the cheese is melted. Remove from the heat; set aside.

In a bowl, combine the flour, baking powder, dill and salt. Cut in butter until mixture resembles coarse crumbs. Stir in sour cream to form a soft dough. Divide dough in half. On a well-floured surface, roll out one portion to fit a deep-dish 9-in. pie plate; trim pastry even with edge.

Pour green bean mixture into crust. Roll out remaining pastry; make a lattice crust. Trim, seal and flute edge. In a small bowl, beat the egg and cream; brush over lattice top. Bake at 400° for 25-35 minutes or until golden brown. **Yield:** 8-10 servings.

Good Beans

Instead of cooking green beans in plain water, I add some beef bouillon granules and sugar to give subtle flavor. —*Roberta Pentz Omak, Washington*

Three-Bean Tomato Cups

Three-Bean Tomato Cups

(Pictured above)

Cilantro and cumin give this delightful salad a Mexican flair. Served in hollowed-out tomatoes, the tasty bean blend makes a pretty addition to a ladies' luncheon or special-occasion meal. Garlic lovers might want to add a second clove. —Audrey Green Ballon
Kentwood, Louisiana

- 3/4 **pound fresh green beans, cut into 2-inch pieces**
- 1/2 **pound fresh wax beans, cut into 2-inch pieces**
- 1 **can (15 ounces) black beans, rinsed and drained**
- 1 **medium sweet red pepper, cut into 1-1/2-inch strips**
- 3 **green onions, sliced**
- 1/4 **cup minced fresh cilantro**
- 1/4 **cup olive oil**
- 3 **tablespoons red wine vinegar**
- 1 **teaspoon ground cumin**
- 1 **garlic clove, minced**
- 1/2 **teaspoon salt**
- 1/4 **teaspoon pepper**
- 6 **large firm tomatoes**

Place the green and wax beans in a saucepan and cover with water; bring to a boil. Cook, uncovered, for 8-10 minutes or until crisp-tender. Drain and place in a large bowl. Add the black beans, red pepper, onions and cilantro.

In a jar with a tight-fitting lid, combine the oil, vinegar, cumin, garlic, salt and pepper; shake well. Pour over bean mixture and toss to coat. Cover and refrigerate for 30 minutes.

Cut a 1/4-in. slice off the top of each tomato; scoop out and discard pulp. Using a slotted spoon, fill tomato cups with bean mixture. **Yield:** 6 servings.

Shepherd's Bean Pie

This comforting casserole is chock-full of fresh green and wax beans, carrots, cubed ham and a handful of crunchy almonds in a creamy Swiss cheese sauce. Topped with mashed potatoes, it makes a hearty side dish. —Karen Cleveland, Spring Valley, Minnesota

- 1-1/4 **pounds fresh green beans, cut into 2-inch pieces**
- 1-1/4 **pounds fresh wax beans, cut into 2-inch pieces**
- 3 **medium carrots, cut into 2-inch julienne strips**
- 1/2 **small onion, chopped**
- 1 **teaspoon butter**
- 1 **can (10-3/4 ounces) condensed cream of chicken soup, undiluted**
- 1/2 **cup heavy whipping cream**
- 1/2 **cup chicken broth**
- 3-1/4 **teaspoons dill weed, *divided***
- 6 **ounces cubed fully cooked ham**
- 1-1/2 **cups (6 ounces) shredded Swiss cheese, *divided***
- 1/4 **cup slivered almonds**
- 7 **cups hot mashed potatoes (prepared with milk and butter)**

Place beans and carrots in a saucepan and cover with water; bring to a boil. Cook, uncovered, for 8-10 minutes or until crisp-tender; drain and set aside. In a small skillet, saute onion in butter for 3-4 minutes or until tender.

In a large bowl, whisk soup, cream, broth and 3 teaspoons of dill. Add the beans, carrots and onion; gently stir to coat. Transfer to a greased shallow 3-qt. baking dish. Top with the ham, 1 cup cheese and almonds. Spread mashed potatoes over the top.

Cover and bake at 350° for 30 minutes. Uncover; sprinkle with remaining cheese and dill. Bake 5-10 minutes longer or until heated through and the cheese is melted. **Yield:** 12-15 servings.

Stir-Fried Beef 'n' Beans

Garlic, ginger and soy sauce lend a robust flavor to this meaty marinated dish. This recipe has become a favorite of family and friends...even those who don't usually eat green beans. —Kristine Lowry
Bowling Green, Kentucky

1/4 cup cornstarch
1/2 cup soy sauce
2 tablespoons water
4 teaspoons minced fresh gingerroot
4 garlic cloves, minced
4 tablespoons vegetable oil, *divided*
1 pound boneless beef sirloin steak, cut into 1/4-inch strips
1/2 pound fresh green beans, cut in half lengthwise
1 teaspoon sugar
1/2 teaspoon salt
Hot cooked rice

In a bowl, combine the cornstarch, soy sauce, water, ginger, garlic and 2 tablespoons oil until smooth. Set aside 1/2 cup. Pour the remaining marinade into a large resealable plastic bag; add the beef. Seal bag and turn to coat; refrigerate for 25-30 minutes.

Drain and discard marinade from beef. In a wok or skillet, stir-fry beef in remaining oil for 4-6 minutes or until no longer pink. Remove and keep warm.

In the same skillet, stir-fry the beans, sugar and salt for 15 minutes or until beans are crisp-tender. Stir in the beef and reserved marinade. Bring to a boil; cook and stir for 1-2 minutes or until thickened. Serve over rice. **Yield:** 4 servings.

Mixed Beans with Lime Butter

This is a simple yet delicious way to showcase both green and wax beans. It is best with beans that are fresh from your garden or the farmers market. The lime butter coating really lets the beans' fresh flavor come through. —Lois Fetting, Nelson, Wisconsin

1/2 pound *each* fresh green and wax beans, trimmed
2 tablespoons butter
2 teaspoons snipped fresh dill
2 teaspoons lime juice
1 teaspoon grated lime peel
1/2 teaspoon salt
1/4 teaspoon pepper

Place beans in a saucepan and cover with water; bring to a boil. Cook, uncovered, for 10 minutes or until crisp-tender; drain. Melt butter in a skillet; add the dill, lime juice and peel, salt, pepper and beans. Stir to coat and cook until heated through. **Yield:** 4 servings.

Picnic Beans with Dip

(Pictured below)

Here's a fun way to enjoy fresh-picked beans…with a creamy well-seasoned dip. Try the dip with other vegetables, too, such as broccoli, celery and carrots. —Martha Bergman, Cleveland Heights, Ohio

 Uses less fat, sugar or salt. Includes Nutritional Analysis and Diabetic Exchanges.

1 pound fresh green *and/or* wax beans
1/2 cup mayonnaise
1/2 cup half-and-half cream
6 tablespoons vegetable oil
2 tablespoons white vinegar
1 tablespoon Dijon mustard
1 small onion, quartered
1 teaspoon salt
1/4 teaspoon ground coriander
1/4 teaspoon dried savory
1/4 teaspoon pepper
1/8 teaspoon dried thyme

Place beans in a saucepan and cover with water; bring to a boil. Cook, uncovered, for 8-10 minutes or until crisp-tender. Drain and rinse with cold water. Refrigerate until serving.

In a blender or food processor, combine the remaining ingredients. Cover and process until smooth. Refrigerate for at least 1 hour. Serve with beans for dipping. **Yield:** 1-2/3 cups dip.

Nutritional Analysis: 2 tablespoons of dip (prepared with fat-free mayonnaise and fat-free half-and-half) equals 85 calories, 7 g fat (1 g saturated fat), 1 mg cholesterol, 293 mg sodium, 5 g carbohydrate, 2 g fiber, trace protein. **Diabetic Exchange:** 2 fat.

Picnic Beans with Dip

String Bean Chicken Skillet

(Pictured below)

I started to prepare a chicken stir-fry one day and discovered I was out of frozen snow peas. So I tossed in green beans instead with a few leftover wax beans for color. I've been making the recipe this way ever since.
—Priscilla Gilbert, Indian Harbour Beach, Florida

- **1/2 pound fresh green beans, cut into 2-inch pieces**
- **1/2 pound fresh wax beans, cut into 2-inch pieces**
- **3 boneless skinless chicken breast halves**
- **2 tablespoons vegetable oil**
- **2 tablespoons plus 1-1/2 teaspoons cornstarch**
- **3 tablespoons soy sauce**
- **1 can (8 ounces) pineapple chunks**
- **1 medium sweet red pepper, julienned**
- **1 small onion, thinly sliced**
- **1/4 teaspoon salt**
- **1/4 teaspoon ground ginger**
- **Hot cooked rice**

Place beans in a saucepan and cover with water; bring to a boil. Cook, uncovered, for 3 minutes; drain and set aside. Flatten chicken to 1/4-in. thickness; cut into 1/2-in. strips. In a large skillet, stir-fry chicken in oil for 2-4 minutes or until no longer pink. Remove with a slotted spoon.

In a small bowl, combine cornstarch and soy sauce until smooth. Drain the pineapple, reserving juice; set pineapple aside. Stir the juice into the soy sauce mixture; set aside. In the skillet, stir-fry red pepper and onion for 5 minutes. Add the chicken, beans, pineapple, salt and ginger. Gradually stir in the soy sauce mixture. Bring to a boil; cook and stir for 2 minutes or until thickened. Serve with rice. **Yield:** 6 servings.

String Bean Chicken Skillet

Italian Green Beans

When I was first married, I wasn't a great cook. More than 20 years later, I have many dishes I'm proud of, including this family favorite. Basil, oregano and Romano cheese give these beans their Italian accent. I serve them with broiled steak, pork roast, lamb chops or pork chops. —Andrea Ibzag, Gordon, Wisconsin

- **1 small onion, chopped**
- **2 tablespoons olive oil**
- **2 to 3 garlic cloves, minced**
- **1 can (14-1/2 ounces) stewed tomatoes, coarsely mashed**
- **1/2 cup water**
- **3 tablespoons minced fresh oregano *or* 1 tablespoon dried oregano**
- **4-1/2 teaspoons minced fresh basil *or* 1-1/2 teaspoons dried basil**
- **1 teaspoon sugar**
- **1 teaspoon salt**
- **1/4 to 1/2 teaspoon coarsely ground pepper**
- **2 pounds fresh green beans, cut into 1-inch pieces**
- **2 tablespoons grated Romano *or* Parmesan cheese**

In a small saucepan, saute onion in oil until tender. Add garlic; saute 1 minute longer. Add the tomatoes, water, oregano, basil, sugar, salt and pepper. Bring to a boil. Reduce heat; simmer, uncovered, for 40 minutes.

Meanwhile, place beans in a large saucepan and cover with water; bring to a boil. Cook, uncovered, for 8-10 minutes or until crisp-tender; drain. Add tomato mixture and cheese; cook for 5 minutes or until heated through. **Yield:** 10 servings.

Two-Bean Tomato Bake

Parmesan cheese, basil and garlic spice up this mouth-watering medley of beans, mushrooms, onion and tomato. A crumb topping adds crunch to this veggie bake that's even more flavorful when you use your garden harvest. —Dorothy Rieke, Julian, Nebraska

- **1-1/2 pounds fresh green beans, cut into 2-inch pieces**

1-1/2 pounds fresh wax beans, cut into 2-inch
    pieces
    5 medium tomatoes, peeled and cubed
1/2 pound fresh mushrooms, sliced
    1 medium sweet onion, chopped
  10 tablespoons butter, *divided*
1-1/2 teaspoons minced garlic, *divided*
1-1/2 teaspoons dried basil, *divided*
1-1/2 teaspoons dried oregano, *divided*
    1 teaspoon salt
1-1/2 cups soft bread crumbs
1/3 cup grated Parmesan cheese

Place beans in a large saucepan and cover with water; bring to a boil. Cook, uncovered, for 8-10 minutes or until crisp-tender. Drain; add the tomatoes and set aside.

In a skillet, saute mushrooms and onion in 4 tablespoons butter. Add 1 teaspoon garlic, 1 teaspoon basil, 1 teaspoon oregano and salt. Add to the bean mixture and toss to coat. Spoon into a greased 3-qt. baking dish.

Melt the remaining butter; toss with bread crumbs, Parmesan cheese and remaining garlic, basil and oregano. Sprinkle over bean mixture. Cover and bake at 400° for 20 minutes. Uncover; bake 15 minutes longer or until golden brown. **Yield:** 14-16 servings.

Beans 'n' Greens

Roasted Green Bean Salad

This easy-to-fix salad recipe turns homegrown green beans into something extra special. A tangy dill weed and Dijon mustard vinaigrette coats the crisp-tender beans without overpowering them so the fresh-picked flavor comes through.
    —Kathy Shell
    San Diego, California

  2 pounds fresh green beans
  3 tablespoons olive oil, *divided*
3/4 teaspoon salt, *divided*
  2 tablespoons white wine vinegar
1-1/2 teaspoons Dijon mustard
  2 tablespoons snipped fresh dill *or* 2
    teaspoons dill weed
1-1/2 teaspoons sugar
1/4 teaspoon pepper

In a bowl, toss the beans with 1 tablespoon oil and 1/2 teaspoon salt. Spread beans in a single layer in an ungreased 15-in. x 10-in. x 1-in. baking pan. Roast, uncovered, at 400° for 30-40 minutes or until the beans are tender and lightly browned, stirring twice.

Meanwhile, in a small bowl, whisk the vinegar, mustard, dill, sugar, pepper and remaining salt. Slowly whisk in remaining oil. Transfer beans to a large serving bowl. Add vinaigrette and toss to coat. **Yield:** 4-6 servings.

Beans 'n' Greens

(Pictured above)

Tasty and a snap to make, this side dish is a guaranteed salad bar star. The tangy marinade dresses up the green beans, spinach and lettuce nicely. I keep the recipe at the front of my easy-to-make file for those nights I need to make supper in a hurry.
    —Dorothy Pritchett, Wills Point, Texas

    1 cup olive oil
  1/4 cup vinegar
1-1/2 teaspoons salt
1-1/2 teaspoons sugar
  1/2 teaspoon celery seed
  1/2 teaspoon paprika
    2 cans (14-1/2 ounces *each*) cut green
    beans, drained *or* 4 cups cooked cut
    fresh green beans (2-inch pieces)
    8 cups torn lettuce
    4 cups torn fresh spinach
    2 cups (8 ounces) shredded Swiss
    cheese

In a jar with a tight-fitting lid, combine oil, vinegar, salt, sugar, celery seed and paprika; shake well. Pour over green beans; let stand for 15 minutes. Just before serving, drain beans, reserving the marinade.

In a salad bowl, combine the beans, lettuce, spinach and Swiss cheese. Drizzle with the reserved marinade and toss to coat. **Yield:** 14-18 servings.

Strawberry Tossed Salad
Tunnel of Berries Cake
Strawberry Swirls
Fresh Strawberry Pie

Chapter 5
Berries

Strawberry Tossed Salad

(Pictured at left)

One reason I particularly like this recipe is that it's so versatile. I've served the salad with poultry, ham and pork throughout the year and even used it to add color to the table at Christmas. —Patricia McNamara
Kansas City, Missouri

1/2 cup vegetable oil
1/3 cup sugar
1/4 cup red wine vinegar
1 garlic clove, minced
1/4 teaspoon salt
1/4 teaspoon paprika
Pinch white pepper
8 cups torn romaine
4 cups torn Bibb *or* Boston lettuce
2-1/2 cups sliced fresh strawberries
1 cup (4 ounces) shredded Monterey Jack cheese
1/2 cup chopped walnuts, toasted

Combine the first seven ingredients in a jar with a tight-fitting lid; shake well. Just before serving, toss the salad greens, strawberries, cheese and walnuts in a large salad bowl. Drizzle with dressing and toss. **Yield:** 6-8 servings.

Fresh Strawberry Pie

(Pictured at left)

Whether I've served this pie at family meals or club luncheons, I have never met a person who didn't enjoy it. It is easy to prepare, tasty and very pretty.
—Florence Robinson, Lenox, Iowa

3/4 cup all-purpose flour
1/2 cup quick-cooking oats
1/2 cup chopped pecans
2 tablespoons sugar
1/8 teaspoon salt
1/2 cup butter, melted

FILLING:
3/4 cup sugar
2 tablespoons cornstarch
1 cup water
2 tablespoons light corn syrup
2 tablespoons strawberry gelatin powder
1 quart fresh strawberries
Whipped cream, optional

In a bowl, combine the flour, oats, pecans, sugar and salt; stir in the butter until blended. Press onto the bottom and up the sides of a 9-in. pie plate. Bake at 400° for 12-15 minutes or until lightly browned. Cool on a wire rack.

Meanwhile, combine sugar and cornstarch in a saucepan. Gradually add water and corn syrup; bring to a boil over medium heat. Cook and stir 2 minutes. Remove from heat; stir in gelatin until dissolved. Cool to room temperature.

Arrange berries in the crust. Carefully pour gelatin mixture over berries. Refrigerate for 2 hours or until set. Serve with whipped cream if desired. **Yield:** 6-8 servings.

Strawberry Secrets

It's best to pick strawberries when they are firm and red. However, berries that are a little green will ripen if you leave them on the kitchen counter for a day.
—Peggy Sue Ulrey, Virginia Beach, Virginia

Since strawberries are fragile, use small shallow containers when picking to avoid crushing them. —Janice Pond
Ludlow, New Brunswick

When I want to quickly cut fresh strawberries into perfectly even slices, I use an egg slicer. —Marsha Rutland, Ovalo, Texas

Using a pastry blender for mashing strawberries is much quicker than using a fork.
—Beverly Grubrich, Novinger, Missouri

Oat-Fashioned
Strawberry Dessert

Oat-Fashioned Strawberry Dessert

(Pictured above)

Thanks to this dessert, our house is a popular place in summertime. I make it for family get-togethers, picnics and potlucks. It's a treat on a breakfast or brunch buffet also. We like it best with whipped cream or a scoop of vanilla ice cream on top.
—Linda Forrest, Belleville, Ontario

> **4 cups sliced fresh strawberries**
> **1-1/4 cups whole wheat flour**
> **1-1/4 cups quick-cooking oats**
> **2/3 cup packed brown sugar**
> **1/4 teaspoon baking soda**
> **1/8 teaspoon salt**
> **2/3 cup cold butter**
> **2 tablespoons sugar**
> **1/4 to 1/2 teaspoon ground cinnamon**

Drain strawberries on paper towels; set aside. In a large bowl, combine flour, oats, brown sugar, baking soda and salt. Cut in butter until mixture resembles coarse crumbs. Reserve 1-1/2 cups for topping. Pat the remaining crumb mixture into a greased 9-in. square baking pan.

In a bowl, combine sugar and cinnamon; stir in strawberries. Spoon over the prepared crust. Sprinkle with the reserved crumb mixture. Bake at 350° for 35-40 minutes or until golden brown. Serve warm. **Yield:** 9 servings.

Tunnel of Berries Cake

(Pictured on page 30)

This cake goes a long way. While it's not overly sweet or heavy, its rich taste makes just one piece very satisfying. *—Shirley Noe, Lebanon Junction, Kentucky*

> **6 eggs, *separated***
> **3/4 cup water**
> **1/2 cup vegetable oil**
> **1-1/2 teaspoons vanilla extract, *divided***
> **2-1/4 cups cake flour**
> **2 cups sugar, *divided***
> **1 tablespoon baking powder**
> **1 teaspoon ground cinnamon**
> **3/4 teaspoon salt**
> **1/4 teaspoon cream of tartar**
> **4 cups fresh whole strawberries, *divided***
> **2-1/2 cups heavy whipping cream**

In a small bowl, combine the egg yolks, water, oil and 1 teaspoon of vanilla; set aside. In a mixing bowl, combine flour, 1 cup sugar, baking powder, cinnamon and salt. Gradually add egg yolk mixture, beating just until smooth.

In another mixing bowl, beat egg whites until foamy. Add cream of tartar; beat until soft peaks form. Fold into batter. Pour into an ungreased 10-in. tube pan. Cut through batter with a knife. Bake at 325° for 60-70 minutes or until top springs back when lightly touched and cracks feel dry.

Immediately invert cake; cool completely. Remove from pan. Slice off top 1/2 in. of cake; set aside. With a knife, cut a tunnel about 1-1/2 in. deep in top of cake, leaving a 3/4-in. shell. Remove cake from tunnel; save for another use.

Chop half of the strawberries; set aside. In a mixing bowl, beat whipping cream until soft peaks form. Gradually add the remaining sugar and vanilla, beating until stiff peaks form. Combine 1-1/2 cups cream mixture and chopped berries; fill the tunnel. Replace cake top. Frost cake with the remaining cream mixture. Refrigerate. Just before serving, cut the remaining strawberries in half and use to garnish the cake. **Yield:** 12 servings.

Blueberry Tea Bread

I have been baking this scrumptious bread for my family over 20 years now. *—Dorothy Simpson*
Blackwood, New Jersey

> **2 cups all-purpose flour**
> **1 cup sugar**
> **1 tablespoon baking powder**

1/4 teaspoon salt
1-1/2 cups fresh *or* frozen blueberries
1 teaspoon grated orange peel
2 eggs
1 cup milk
3 tablespoons vegetable oil
Whipped cream cheese, optional

In a bowl, combine flour, sugar, baking powder and salt. Stir in blueberries and orange peel. In another bowl, beat eggs; add milk and oil. Stir into dry ingredients just until moistened.

Pour into a greased 9-in. x 5-in. x 3-in. loaf pan. Bake at 350° for 1 hour or until a toothpick comes out clean. Cool in pan for 10 minutes; remove to a wire rack to cool completely. Serve with cream cheese if desired. **Yield:** 1 loaf.

Strawberry Swirls

(Pictured on page 30)

My mother-in-law's apple cobbler was the inspiration for my variation. And it is amazing how many family members and friends "pop over" during strawberry season! —Paula Steele, Obion, Tennessee

2 cups sugar
2 cups water
1/2 cup butter, melted
1/2 cup shortening
1-1/2 cups self-rising flour
1/2 cup milk
2 cups finely chopped fresh strawberries, drained
Whipped cream, optional

In a saucepan, combine sugar and water; cook and stir over medium heat until sugar is dissolved. Remove from the heat; allow to cool. Pour butter into a 13-in. x 9-in. x 2-in. baking dish; set aside. In a bowl, cut shortening into flour until mixture resembles coarse crumbs. Stir in milk until moistened.

Turn onto a lightly floured surface; knead until smooth, about 8-10 times. Roll into a 12-in. x 8-in. rectangle; sprinkle with the strawberries. Roll up, jelly-roll style, starting with a long side; seal the seam. Cut into 12 slices. Place with cut side down over butter. Carefully pour syrup around rolls. Bake at 350° for 40-45 minutes or until golden brown and edges are bubbly. Serve warm with whipped cream if desired. **Yield:** 12 servings.

Editor's Note: As a substitute for the 1-1/2 cups of self-rising flour called for in this recipe, place 1-1/2 teaspoons baking powder and 1/2 teaspoon salt in a 1-cup measuring cup; add enough all-purpose flour to equal 1 cup. Then place 3/4 teaspoon baking powder and 1/4 teaspoon salt in a 1/2-cup measuring cup; add all-purpose flour to equal 1/2 cup.

Strawberries 'n' Cream Bread

(Pictured below)

Once strawberry-picking time arrives here each summer, my husband and I look forward to this bread. Since only fresh strawberries will do, I have been thinking of trying a different kind of berry so we can enjoy it more often. —Suzanne Randall, Dexter, Maine

1/2 cup butter, softened
3/4 cup sugar
2 eggs
1/2 cup sour cream
1 teaspoon vanilla extract
1-3/4 cups all-purpose flour
1/2 teaspoon baking powder
1/2 teaspoon baking soda
1/2 teaspoon salt
1/4 teaspoon ground cinnamon
3/4 cup chopped fresh strawberries
3/4 cup chopped walnuts, toasted, *divided*

In a mixing bowl, cream butter and sugar until fluffy. Beat in eggs, one at a time. Add sour cream and vanilla; mix well. Combine the flour, baking powder, baking soda, salt and cinnamon; stir into creamed mixture just until moistened. Fold in strawberries and 1/2 cup nuts.

Pour into a greased 8-in. x 4-in. x 2-in. loaf pan. Sprinkle with remaining nuts. Bake at 350° for 65-70 minutes or until a toothpick inserted near the center comes out clean. Cool for 10 minutes; remove from pan to a wire rack to cool completely. **Yield:** 1 loaf.

Strawberries 'n' Cream Bread

Blackberry Fizz

(Pictured below)

For a festive beverage with a distinctive berry flavor and a hint of spice, try this recipe. We save it for holidays and special times with family and friends. It's a delightful drink people will remember.
—Andrea Eberly, Sarasota, Florida

3 quarts fresh *or* frozen blackberries
4 cups water
3 cups sugar
1 tablespoon whole cloves
1 tablespoon whole allspice
2 cinnamon sticks (4 inches), broken
Lemon-lime *or* white soda

Crush blackberries in a large kettle. Add water and bring to a boil. Reduce heat to medium and cook for 10 minutes. Strain through a jelly bag, reserving juice and discarding pulp. Add water to juice if necessary to equal 2 quarts; pour into a large kettle. Slowly stir in sugar until dissolved. Place spices in a cheesecloth bag; add to juice. Simmer, uncovered, for 30 minutes. Bring to a boil; remove the spice bag and discard.

Pour hot into hot jars, leaving 1/4-in. headspace. Adjust caps. Process for 15 minutes in a boiling-water bath. To serve, mix about one-third concentrate with two-thirds soda. **Yield:** about 4 pints concentrate.

Blackberry Fizz

Super Strawberry Shortcake

"Wow!" is what people say when I set this dessert on the table. It's fun to serve since it's attractive and bursting with the wondrous flavor of field-fresh strawberries.
—Renee Bisch, Wellesley, Ontario

1 quart fresh strawberries, sliced
1 to 2 tablespoons sugar
SHORTCAKE:
1-3/4 cups all-purpose flour
2 tablespoons sugar
1 tablespoon baking powder
1/2 teaspoon baking soda
1/2 teaspoon salt
1/4 cup cold butter
1 egg
3/4 cup sour cream
TOPPING:
1 cup heavy whipping cream
1 to 2 tablespoons sugar
1 teaspoon vanilla extract

Combine the strawberries and sugar; set aside. For shortcake, combine dry ingredients in a large bowl; cut in butter until crumbly. In a small bowl, beat egg; add sour cream. Stir into the crumb mixture just until moistened.

Turn onto a floured surface; knead 25 times or until smooth. Roll out into a 7-1/2-in. circle. Cut a 2-in. hole in center to form a ring. Place on a lightly greased baking sheet. Bake at 425° for 12-14 minutes or until golden. Remove from baking sheet; cool on a wire rack.

For topping, beat cream and sugar until stiff peaks form; stir in vanilla. Just before serving, split cake horizontally. Spoon juice from berries over bottom layer. Spoon half of berries over juice. Spread half of topping over berries. Add the top cake layer, remaining topping and berries. Cut into wedges. **Yield:** 8 servings.

Glazed Blackberry Pie

I always use the first ripe blackberries of the season to make this simple fruit pie. *—Monica Gross Downey, California*

5 cups fresh blackberries, *divided*
1 pastry shell (9 inches), baked
1 cup water, *divided*
3/4 cup sugar
3 tablespoons cornstarch
Red food coloring, optional
Whipped topping

Place 2 cups blackberries in pastry shell; set aside. In a saucepan, crush 1 cup berries. Add 3/4 cup water. Bring to a boil over medium heat, stirring constantly. Cook and stir for 2 minutes. Press berries through a sieve. Set juice aside; discard pulp.

In a saucepan, combine the sugar and cornstarch. Stir in remaining water and reserved juice until smooth. Bring to a boil; cook and stir for 2 minutes or until thickened. Remove from the heat; stir in food coloring if desired. Pour half of the glaze over berries in pastry shell. Stir remaining berries into remaining glaze; carefully spoon over filling.

Refrigerate for 3 hours or until set. Garnish with whipped topping. Refrigerate leftovers. **Yield:** 6-8 servings.

Blueberry-Peach Pound Cake

I was going to make apple pound cake for my husband's birthday but found I had no apples. I had picked up blueberries and peaches from a local grower, so I decided to use them instead. —Nancy Zimmerman
Cape May Court House, New Jersey

1/2 cup butter, softened
1-1/4 cups sugar
3 eggs
1/4 cup milk
2-1/2 cups cake flour
2 teaspoons baking powder
1/4 teaspoon salt
2-1/4 cups chopped peeled fresh peaches
2 cups fresh *or* frozen blueberries
Confectioners' sugar, optional

In a mixing bowl, cream butter and sugar. Beat in eggs, one at a time. Beat in milk. Combine the flour, baking powder and salt; add to creamed mixture. Stir in peaches and blueberries.

Pour into a greased and floured 10-in. fluted tube pan. Bake at 350° for 60-70 minutes or until a toothpick inserted near the center comes out clean. Cool in pan for 15 minutes; remove to a wire rack to cool completely. Dust with confectioners' sugar if desired. **Yield:** 10-12 servings.

Blueberry Basics

Look for blueberries that are firm, dry, plump, smooth-skinned and free of leaves and stems. Avoid berry containers with juice stains, which may be a sign that the berries are crushed and possibly moldy.
—*Anna Higbee, Absecon, New Jersey*

Raspberry-Cranberry Soup

Raspberry-Cranberry Soup

(Pictured above)

Served hot, this beautiful tangy soup helps beat the winter "blahs". On a sunny summer day, it's refreshing cold. I have fun serving it because people are so intrigued with the idea of a fruit soup. —Susan Stull
Chillicothe, Missouri

2 cups fresh *or* frozen cranberries
2 cups apple juice
1 cup fresh *or* frozen unsweetened
raspberries, thawed
1/2 to 1 cup sugar
1 tablespoon lemon juice
1/4 teaspoon ground cinnamon
2 cups half-and-half cream, *divided*
1 tablespoon cornstarch
Whipped cream, additional raspberries and
mint, optional

In a 3-qt. saucepan, bring cranberries and apple juice to a boil. Reduce heat and simmer, uncovered, for 10 minutes. Press through a sieve; return to the pan. Also press the raspberries through the sieve; discard skins and seeds. Add to cranberry mixture; bring to a boil. Add sugar, lemon juice and cinnamon; remove from the heat.

Cool 4 minutes. Stir 1 cup into 1-1/2 cups cream. Return all to pan; bring to a gentle boil. Mix cornstarch with remaining cream; stir into soup. Cook and stir for 2 minutes. Serve hot or chilled. Garnish with whipped cream, raspberries and mint if desired. **Yield:** 4 servings.

Raspberry Ribbon Cheesecake

Raspberry Ribbon Cheesecake

(Pictured above)

Here's a mouth-watering dessert that's sure to impress family and friends. It tastes wonderful with its chocolate cookie crust, rich creamy cheesecake and tangy raspberry center and topping. —Peggy Frasier
Indianapolis, Indiana

     2 cups chocolate wafer crumbs
 1/3 cup butter, melted
     3 tablespoons sugar
RASPBERRY SAUCE:
2-1/2 cups fresh *or* frozen unsweetened
         raspberries, thawed
 2/3 cup sugar
     2 tablespoons cornstarch
     2 teaspoons lemon juice
FILLING/TOPPING:
     3 packages (8 ounces *each*) cream
         cheese, softened
 1/2 cup sugar
     2 tablespoons all-purpose flour
     1 teaspoon vanilla extract
     2 egg whites
     1 cup heavy whipping cream
     2 to 3 tablespoons orange juice
1-1/2 cups fresh *or* frozen unsweetened
         raspberries, thawed

Combine the first three ingredients; press into bottom and 1-1/2 in. up sides of a greased 9-in. springform pan. Chill 1 hour or until firm. Puree raspberries in a blender or food processor. Press through a sieve; discard seeds. Add water if necessary to measure 1 cup. In a saucepan, combine sugar and cornstarch. Stir in raspberry juice; bring to a boil. Boil 2 minutes, stirring constantly. Remove from heat; stir in lemon juice and set aside.

In a mixing bowl, beat cream cheese, sugar, flour and vanilla until fluffy. Add egg whites; beat on low just until blended. Stir in cream. Pour half into crust. Top with 3/4 cup raspberry sauce (cover and refrigerate remaining sauce). Carefully spoon remaining filling over sauce.

Bake at 375° for 35-40 minutes or until center is nearly set. Remove from oven; immediately run a knife around pan to loosen crust. Cool on wire rack 1 hour. Refrigerate overnight. Add orange juice to chilled raspberry sauce; gently fold in raspberries. Spoon over the cheesecake. **Yield:** 12-16 servings.

Summertime Strawberry Gelatin Salad

For years, this salad has been a "must" at family dinners and special occasions. It's as pretty as it is good.
—Janet England, Chillicothe, Missouri

     1 package (3 ounces) strawberry gelatin
     1 cup boiling water
     1 cup cold water
MIDDLE LAYER:
     1 envelope unflavored gelatin
 1/2 cup cold water
     1 cup half-and-half cream
     1 package (8 ounces) cream cheese,
         softened
     1 cup sugar
 1/2 teaspoon vanilla extract
TOP LAYER:
     1 package (6 ounces) strawberry gelatin
     1 cup boiling water
     1 cup cold water
     3 to 4 cups sliced fresh strawberries

In a bowl, dissolve strawberry gelatin in boiling water; stir in cold water. Pour into a 13-in. x 9-in. x 2-in. dish; chill until set.

Meanwhile, place unflavored gelatin and cold water in a small bowl; let stand until softened. In a saucepan over medium heat, heat cream (do not boil). Add softened gelatin; stir until gelatin is dissolved. Cool to room temperature. In a mixing bowl, beat cream cheese, sugar and vanilla until smooth. Gradually add unflavored gelatin mixture; mix well. Carefully pour over bottom layer. Refrigerate until set, about 1 hour.

For top layer, dissolve strawberry gelatin in boiling water; stir in cold water. Cool to room temperature. Stir in strawberries; carefully spoon over middle layer. Refrigerate overnight. **Yield:** 12-16 servings.

Editor's Note: This salad takes time to prepare since each layer must be set before the next layer is added.

Strawberry Melon Fizz

Experimenting in the kitchen's fun for me. That's how I came up with this—I adapted it from two different recipes I got from friends for a melon ball basket and for a sparkling beverage.
—*Teresa Messick*
Montgomery, Alabama

     2 cups sugar
     1 cup water
     5 fresh mint sprigs
     1 quart fresh strawberries, halved
     2 cups cubed honeydew
 1-3/4 cups cubed cantaloupe
 Ginger ale *or* sparkling white grape juice

In a saucepan, combine the sugar, water and mint; bring to a boil. Boil and stir until a candy thermometer reads 240° (soft-ball stage). Remove from the heat; allow to cool. Discard mint.

Combine the strawberries and melon. Just before serving, fill tall glasses with fruit and drizzle with 1 tablespoon syrup. Add ginger ale to each. **Yield:** 8-10 servings.

Blueberry French Toast

(Pictured at right)

This is the best breakfast dish I've ever tasted. With luscious blueberries inside and in a sauce that drizzles over each slice, it's almost a dessert. The recipe was shared with me by a local blueberry grower.
—*Patricia Walls, Aurora, Minnesota*

 12 slices day-old white bread, crusts
         removed
     2 packages (8 ounces *each*) cream cheese
     1 cup fresh *or* frozen blueberries
 12 eggs
     2 cups milk
 1/3 cup maple syrup *or* honey
 SAUCE:
     1 cup sugar
     2 tablespoons cornstarch
     1 cup water
     1 cup fresh *or* frozen blueberries
     1 tablespoon butter

Cut bread into 1-in. cubes; place half in a greased 13-in. x 9-in. x 2-in. baking dish. Cut cream cheese into 1-in. cubes; place over bread. Top with blueberries and remaining bread. In a large bowl, beat eggs. Add milk and syrup; mix well. Pour over bread mixture. Cover and chill 8 hours or overnight. Remove from refrigerator 30 minutes before baking.

Cover and bake at 350° for 30 minutes. Uncover; bake 25-30 minutes more or until golden brown and the center is set.

In a saucepan, combine sugar and cornstarch; add water. Bring to a boil over medium heat; boil for 3 minutes, stirring constantly. Stir in blueberries; reduce heat. Simmer for 8-10 minutes or until berries have burst. Stir in butter until melted. Serve over French toast. **Yield:** 6-8 servings (1-3/4 cups sauce).

Fresh Raspberry Pie

Mouth-watering fresh raspberries star in this luscious pie. There's nothing to distract from the tangy berry flavor and gorgeous ruby color. A big slice is an excellent way to enjoy the taste of summer.
—*Patricia Staudt, Marble Rock, Iowa*

 1/4 cup sugar
     1 tablespoon cornstarch
     1 cup water
     1 package (3 ounces) raspberry gelatin
     4 cups fresh raspberries
     1 graham cracker crust (9 inches)

In a saucepan, combine sugar and cornstarch. Add the water and bring to a boil, stirring constantly. Cook and stir for 2 minutes. Remove from the heat; stir in gelatin until dissolved. Cool for 15 minutes. Place raspberries in the crust; slowly pour gelatin mixture over berries. Chill until set, about 3 hours. **Yield:** 6-8 servings.

Blueberry French Toast

Four-Berry Spread

Four-Berry Spread

(Pictured above)

For a big berry taste, you can't beat this tasty spread. With a flavorful foursome of blackberries, blueberries, raspberries and strawberries, this lovely jam brightens any breakfast. —Marie St. Thomas
Sterling, Massachusetts

 1 cup fresh *or* frozen blackberries
 1 cup fresh *or* frozen blueberries
1-1/2 cups fresh *or* frozen strawberries
1-1/2 cups fresh *or* frozen raspberries
 1 box (1-3/4 ounces) powdered fruit pectin
 7 cups sugar

Crush berries in a large kettle. Stir in pectin; bring to a full rolling boil over high heat, stirring constantly. Stir in sugar; return to a full rolling boil. Boil for 1 minute, stirring constantly. Remove from the heat; skim off any foam.

Pour hot into hot jars, leaving 1/4-in. headspace. Adjust caps. Process for 10 minutes in a boiling-water bath. **Yield:** about 7 half-pints.

Raspberry Crumb Cake

A cake spiced with cinnamon and mace and a yummy raspberry filling assure this treat will brighten any buffet. Folks will be back for seconds. —Pat Habiger
Spearville, Kansas

 2/3 cup sugar
 1/4 cup cornstarch
 3/4 cup water
 2 cups fresh *or* frozen unsweetened
 raspberries
 1 tablespoon lemon juice
CRUST:
 3 cups all-purpose flour
 1 cup sugar
 1 tablespoon baking powder
 1 teaspoon salt
 1 teaspoon ground cinnamon
 1/4 teaspoon ground mace
 1 cup cold butter
 2 eggs
 1 cup milk
 1 teaspoon vanilla extract

TOPPING:
  1/2 cup all-purpose flour
  1/2 cup sugar
  1/4 cup cold butter
  1/4 cup sliced almonds

In a saucepan, combine sugar, cornstarch, water and raspberries. Bring to a boil over medium heat; boil for 5 minutes or until thickened, stirring constantly. Remove from heat; stir in lemon juice. Cool.

Meanwhile, in a bowl, combine first six crust ingredients. Cut in butter until mixture resembles coarse crumbs. Beat eggs, milk and vanilla; add to crumb mixture and mix well. Spread two-thirds of mixture into a greased 13-in. x 9-in. x 2-in. baking dish. Spoon raspberry filling over crust to within 1 in. of edges. Top with remaining crust mixture.

For topping, combine flour and sugar; cut in butter until crumbly. Stir in almonds. Sprinkle over the top. Bake at 350° for 50-55 minutes or until lightly browned. **Yield:** 12-16 servings.

Refreshing Raspberry Cooler

Here's one thirst-quenching way to enjoy the goodness of raspberries in a glass. —Doreen Patterson
Qualicum Beach, British Columbia

  8 cups fresh *or* frozen raspberries, thawed
1-1/2 cups sugar
  2/3 cup cider vinegar
  1/2 cup water
  2 liters ginger ale, chilled
  2 cups cold water

In a large saucepan, crush the berries. Stir in sugar, vinegar and water. Bring to a boil; reduce heat. Simmer, uncovered, for 20 minutes. Strain to remove seeds; refrigerate. Just before serving, stir in ginger ale and cold water. Serve over ice. **Yield:** about 3-1/2 quarts.

Berry Good Ice Cream Sauce

I started cooking in earnest as a bride over 40 years ago. I'm thankful to say I improved in time.
—Joy Beck, Cincinnati, Ohio

1-3/4 cups sliced fresh *or* frozen rhubarb
  2/3 cup pureed fresh *or* frozen strawberries
  1/4 cup sugar
  1/4 cup orange juice
  2 cups sliced fresh *or* frozen strawberries
Vanilla ice cream

In a saucepan, combine the first four ingredients. Cook over medium heat until rhubarb is tender, about 5 minutes. Stir in the sliced strawberries. Store in the refrigerator. Serve over ice cream. **Yield:** 3-1/2 cups.

Summer Berry Pie

(Pictured below)

Mom puts luscious fresh blueberries, strawberries and raspberries to great use in this cool, refreshing pie. A super dessert on a hot day, it provides a nice light ending to a hearty meal. —Judi Messina
Coeur d'Alene, Idaho

1-1/2 cups sugar
  6 tablespoons cornstarch
  3 cups cold water
  1 package (6 ounces) raspberry *or* strawberry gelatin
  2 cups fresh blueberries
  2 cups sliced fresh strawberries
  2 cups fresh raspberries
  2 graham cracker crusts (9 inches)
  4 cups whipped topping
Fresh mint and additional sliced strawberries

In a saucepan, combine sugar, cornstarch and water until smooth. Bring to a boil; cook and stir for 2 minutes or until thickened. Remove from the heat. Stir in gelatin until dissolved. Refrigerate for 15-20 minutes or until mixture begins to thicken.

Stir in the berries. Pour into crusts and chill until set. Garnish with whipped topping, mint and strawberries. **Yield:** 2 pies (6-8 servings each).

Summer Berry Pie

Lemon Whirligigs with Raspberries

(Pictured below)

Golden whirligigs with a tart lemon flavor float on a ruby raspberry sauce in this delectable dessert. I love serving it for guests. My children also like it made with blackberries.
—Vicki Ayres
Wappingers Falls, New York

2/3 cup sugar
2 tablespoons cornstarch
1/4 teaspoon ground cinnamon
1/8 teaspoon ground nutmeg
1/8 teaspoon salt
1 cup water
3 cups fresh raspberries
WHIRLIGIGS:
1 cup all-purpose flour
2 teaspoons baking powder
1/2 teaspoon salt
3 tablespoons shortening
1 egg, lightly beaten
2 tablespoons half-and-half cream
1/4 cup sugar
2 tablespoons butter, melted
1 teaspoon grated lemon peel
Heavy whipping cream and additional raspberries, optional

In a saucepan, combine sugar, cornstarch, cinnamon, nutmeg and salt. Gradually add water; bring to a boil. Reduce heat to medium; cook and stir until the sauce thickens, about 5 minutes. Place berries in an ungreased 1-1/2-qt. shallow baking dish; pour hot sauce over top. Bake at 400° for 10 minutes; remove from the oven and set aside.

For whirligigs, combine first three ingredients in

Lemon Whirligigs With Raspberries

a bowl; cut in shortening until crumbly. Combine egg and cream; stir into dry ingredients to form a stiff dough. Shape into a ball; place on a lightly floured surface. Roll into a 12-in. x 6-in. rectangle. Combine sugar, butter and lemon peel; spread over dough. Roll up jelly roll style, starting at a long side. Cut into 10 slices; pat each slice to flatten slightly. Place on top of berry mixture.

Bake at 400° for 15 minutes or until whirligigs are golden. Garnish servings with cream and raspberries if desired. **Yield:** 10 servings.

Berry Apple Crumble

You can serve this crumble as a snack, and it's also great for a breakfast gathering or church supper. It is good hot and good on the second day as well.
—Ginger Isham, Williston, Vermont

8 to 10 tart apples, peeled and sliced
2 tablespoons cornstarch
1 can (12 ounces) frozen apple juice concentrate, thawed
2 tablespoons butter
1 teaspoon ground cinnamon
1 teaspoon lemon juice
1 cup fresh *or* frozen blackberries
1 cup fresh *or* frozen raspberries
TOPPING:
2 cups quick-cooking oats
1/2 cup all-purpose flour
1/2 cup chopped walnuts
1/3 cup vegetable oil
1/3 cup maple syrup

Place the apples in a greased 13-in. x 9-in. x 2-in. baking dish; set aside. In a saucepan, combine cornstarch and apple juice. Bring to a boil; cook and stir for 2 minutes or until thickened. Add butter, cinnamon and lemon juice. Pour over the apples. Sprinkle with berries. In a bowl, combine the oats, flour and walnuts; add oil and syrup. Sprinkle over berries. Bake at 350° for 40-45 minutes or until filling is bubbly and topping is golden brown. **Yield: 10-12 servings.**

Blueberry Cream Pie

Whenever I ask my family which pie they'd like me to make, everyone gives the same answer—Blueberry Cream Pie! This refreshing dessert has an enticing cream layer topped with lots of plump blueberries.
—Kim Erickson, Sturgis, Michigan

1-1/3 cups vanilla wafer crumbs
    2 tablespoons sugar
    5 tablespoons butter, melted
    1/2 teaspoon vanilla extract
FILLING:
    1/4 cup sugar
    3 tablespoons all-purpose flour
Pinch salt
    1 cup half-and-half cream
    3 egg yolks, beaten
    3 tablespoons butter
    1 teaspoon vanilla extract
    1 tablespoon confectioners' sugar
TOPPING:
    5 cups fresh blueberries, *divided*
    2/3 cup sugar
    1 tablespoon cornstarch

Combine the first four ingredients; press into the bottom and sides of an ungreased 9-in. pie pan. Bake at 350° for 8-10 minutes or until crust just begins to brown. Cool.

In a saucepan, combine sugar, flour and salt. Gradually whisk in cream; cook and stir over medium heat until thickened and bubbly. Cook and stir 2 minutes more. Gradually whisk half into egg yolks; return all to pan. Bring to a gentle boil; cook and stir 2 minutes. Remove from heat; stir in butter and vanilla until butter is melted. Cool 5 minutes, stirring occasionally. Pour into crust; sprinkle with confectioners' sugar. Chill 30 minutes or until set.

Meanwhile, crush 2 cups of blueberries in a medium saucepan; bring to a boil. Boil 2 minutes, stirring constantly. Press berries through sieve; set aside 1 cup juice (add water if necessary). Discard pulp. In a saucepan, combine sugar and cornstarch. Gradually stir in blueberry juice; bring to a boil. Boil 2 minutes, stirring constantly. Remove from heat; cool 15 minutes. Gently stir in remaining blueberries; carefully spoon over the filling. Chill for 3 hours or until set. Store in the refrigerator. **Yield: 6-8 servings.**

Vanilla Cream Fruit Tart

Vanilla Cream Fruit Tart

(Pictured above)

It's well worth the effort to prepare this spectacular tart, which is best made and served the same day. A friend gave me the recipe.   *—Susan Terzakis*
Andover, Massachusetts

    3/4 cup butter, softened
    1/2 cup confectioners' sugar
1-1/2 cups all-purpose flour
    1 package (10 to 12 ounces) vanilla *or*
    white chips, melted and cooled
    1/4 cup heavy whipping cream
    1 package (8 ounces) cream cheese, softened
    1 pint fresh strawberries, sliced
    1 cup fresh blueberries
    1 cup fresh raspberries
    1/2 cup pineapple juice
    1/4 cup sugar
    1 tablespoon cornstarch
    1/2 teaspoon lemon juice

In a mixing bowl, cream butter and confectioners' sugar. Beat in the flour (mixture will be crumbly). Pat into the bottom of a greased 12-in. pizza pan. Bake at 300° for 25-28 minutes or until lightly browned. Cool.

In another mixing bowl, beat melted chips and cream. Add cream cheese; beat until smooth. Spread over crust. Chill for 30 minutes. Arrange berries over filling.

In a saucepan, combine pineapple juice, sugar, cornstarch and lemon juice; bring to a boil over medium heat. Boil for 2 minutes or until thickened, stirring constantly. Cool; brush over fruit. Chill 1 hour before serving. Store in the refrigerator. **Yield: 12-16 servings.**

Tomato French Bread Lasagna
Fruity Chili Sauce
Tomato Dill Soup
Herbed Cherry Tomatoes

Chapter 6
Tomatoes

Tomato Dill Soup

(Pictured at left and on front cover)

Most often, I make this soup ahead and keep it in the fridge. It's particularly good to take out and heat up with tuna or grilled cheese sandwiches or a salad.
—Patty Kile, Greentown, Pennsylvania

1 medium onion, thinly sliced
1 garlic clove, minced
2 tablespoons vegetable oil
1 tablespoon butter
1/2 teaspoon salt
Pinch pepper
3 large tomatoes, sliced
1 can (6 ounces) tomato paste
1/4 cup all-purpose flour
2 cups water, *divided*
3/4 cup heavy whipping cream, whipped
1 to 2 tablespoons finely minced fresh dill
or 1 to 2 teaspoons dill weed

In a large saucepan over low heat, cook onion and garlic in oil and butter until tender. Add salt, pepper and tomatoes; cook over medium-high heat for 3 minutes. Remove from heat; stir in tomato paste.

In a small bowl, combine flour and 1/2 cup of water; stir until smooth. Stir into saucepan. Gradually stir in remaining water until smooth; bring to a boil over medium heat. Cook and stir for 2 minutes.

Place mixture in a sieve over a bowl. With the back of a spoon, press vegetables through the sieve to remove seeds and skin; return puree to pan. Add cream and dill; cook over low heat just until heated through (do not boil). **Yield:** 4 servings (1 quart).

Tomato French Bread Lasagna

(Pictured at left and on front cover)

Usually, I make this as a side dish to go with veal cutlets or a roast. You could also serve it as a main dish along with a salad and hot garlic bread if you'd like.
—Patricia Collins, Imbler, Oregon

1 pound ground beef
1/3 cup chopped onion
1/3 cup chopped celery
2 garlic cloves, minced
14 slices French bread (1/2 inch thick)
4 large tomatoes, sliced 1/2 inch thick
1 teaspoon dried basil
1 teaspoon dried parsley flakes
1 teaspoon dried oregano
1 teaspoon dried rosemary, crushed
1 teaspoon garlic powder
3/4 teaspoon salt
1/2 teaspoon pepper
2 teaspoons olive oil, *divided*
3 tablespoons butter
3 tablespoons all-purpose flour
1-1/2 cups milk
1/3 cup grated Parmesan cheese
2 cups (8 ounces) shredded mozzarella cheese

In a skillet, cook beef, onion, celery and garlic over medium heat until meat is no longer pink; drain and set aside. Toast bread; line the bottom of an ungreased 13-in. x 9-in. x 2-in. baking dish with 10 slices. Top with half of the meat mixture and half of the tomatoes. Combine seasonings; sprinkle half over tomatoes. Drizzle with 1 teaspoon oil. Crumble remaining bread over top. Repeat layers of meat, tomatoes, seasonings and oil.

In a saucepan over medium heat, melt the butter; stir in flour until smooth. Gradually stir in milk; bring to a boil. Cook and stir until thickened and bubbly, about 2 minutes. Remove from the heat; stir in Parmesan. Pour over casserole. Top with mozzarella. Bake, uncovered, at 350° for 40-45 minutes or until bubbly and cheese is golden brown. **Yield:** 8-10 servings.

Tomato Tip

To season plain hoagies or hamburgers, marinate tomato slices with Italian or French dressing. Top sandwiches just before serving.
—Nancy Ray, Williamsburg, Pennsylvania

Herbed Cherry Tomatoes

(Pictured on page 42 and on front cover)

My recipe's a good one for when you want a little fancier salad dish but one that's still quick to fix. I find it's especially popular served with grilled steak, baked potatoes and corn on the cob. —Dianne Bahn
Yankton, South Dakota

    1 pint cherry tomatoes, halved
  1/4 cup vegetable oil
    3 tablespoons vinegar
  1/4 cup minced fresh parsley
1-1/2 teaspoons minced fresh basil *or* 1/2
    teaspoon dried basil
1-1/2 teaspoons minced fresh oregano *or* 1/2
    teaspoon dried oregano
  1/2 teaspoon salt
  1/2 teaspoon sugar
Leaf lettuce, optional

Place tomatoes in a medium bowl; set aside. In a small bowl, combine oil and vinegar. Add parsley, basil, oregano, salt and sugar; mix well. Pour over the tomatoes. Cover and refrigerate for at least 3 hours. Drain; serve on lettuce if desired. **Yield:** 4-6 servings.

Fruity Chili Sauce

(Pictured on page 42 and on front cover)

Not long ago, I served this with crown roast pork to a group. Everyone loved it and asked me for the recipe.

Southwestern Tomato Soup

My husband and I make the sauce together once a year—around late August, when the fruits and vegetables are ripe and ready in our part of the country. It stores well. —Kathy Kalyta, Lakefield, Ontario

 20 medium tomatoes, chopped
  6 medium onions, chopped
  5 medium ripe peaches, peeled and
    chopped
  5 medium ripe pears, chopped
  1 medium green pepper, chopped
  1 medium sweet red pepper, chopped
  4 cups sugar
  1 cup vinegar
  2 tablespoons salt
1/4 cup mixed pickling spices

In a large kettle, combine the first nine ingredients; bring to a boil. Reduce heat to simmer. Tie pickling spices in a double thickness of cheesecloth; add to the tomato mixture. Simmer, uncovered, for 1-1/2 hours or until volume is reduced by half, stirring frequently. Discard the spice bag.

    Store in the refrigerator for up to 2 months or ladle hot into hot jars, leaving 1/4-in. headspace. Adjust caps. Process for 15 minutes in a boiling-water bath. Serve over cooked pork, chicken or turkey. **Yield:** about 8 pints.

Southwestern Tomato Soup

(Pictured at left)

This smooth, flavorful tomato soup is unbeatable when the season's ripest tomatoes are available and the weather starts to cool. Each delicious, fresh-tasting bowlful will warm you from the inside out.
—Sherri Jackson, Chillicothe, Ohio

 10 plum tomatoes, halved lengthwise
  1 to 2 Anaheim peppers, halved and
    seeded
1/2 cup chopped onion
  2 garlic cloves, minced
  1 tablespoon olive oil
  2 cans (14-1/2 ounces *each*) chicken
    broth
  1 tablespoon minced fresh cilantro
  2 teaspoons ground cumin
1/2 teaspoon sugar
1/2 teaspoon salt
1/4 teaspoon pepper
Vegetable oil for frying
  8 corn tortillas (6 inches), cut into 1/4-inch
    strips
Sour cream, optional

Place tomatoes cut side down on a broiler pan; broil 3-4 in. from the heat for 15-20 minutes. Peel and discard skins. Repeat with peppers, broiling for 5-10 minutes.

In a skillet, saute onion and garlic in oil until tender. Transfer to a blender or food processor; add the tomatoes and peppers. Cover and process until smooth. Pour into a large saucepan; cook and stir over medium heat for 2 minutes.

Press mixture through a strainer with a spoon; discard seeds. Return tomato mixture to the pan. Add broth, cilantro, cumin, sugar, salt and pepper. Cover and cook on low for 15-20 minutes or until heated through.

Meanwhile, heat 1/2 in. of oil in a skillet to 375°. Fry tortilla strips, in batches, for 3-5 minutes or until golden brown; drain on paper towels. Garnish bowls of soup with tortilla strips. Serve with sour cream if desired. **Yield:** 6 servings.

Editor's Note: When cutting and seeding hot peppers, use rubber or plastic gloves to protect your hands; avoid touching your face.

Tomato-Onion Phyllo Pizza

Tomato Crouton Casserole

This baked dish uses lots of garden-fresh, delicious tomatoes and seasonings that give it an Italian twist. Every time I serve this dish, someone asks for a copy of the recipe. —Norma Nelson, Punta Gorda, Florida

    8 medium tomatoes, peeled and cut into
       wedges
    8 slices bread, crusts removed and cubed
 1/2 cup plus 2 tablespoons butter, melted
    1 teaspoon salt
    1 teaspoon dried basil
    1 teaspoon dried thyme
 3/4 cup grated Parmesan cheese

Arrange tomatoes in a greased 13-in. x 9-in. x 2-in. baking dish. Top with bread cubes. Combine butter, salt, basil and thyme; drizzle over bread and tomatoes. Sprinkle with cheese. Bake, uncovered, at 350° for 30-35 minutes or until tomatoes are tender. **Yield:** 8-10 servings.

Tomato-Onion Phyllo Pizza

(Pictured above right)

With a delicate crust and lots of lovely tomatoes on top, this dish is a special one to serve to guests. I make it often when fresh garden tomatoes are in season. It freezes well unbaked, so I can keep one on hand to pop in the oven for a quick dinner. —Neta Cohen, Bedford, Virginia

    5 tablespoons butter, melted
    7 sheets phyllo dough (18 inches x 14
       inches)
    7 tablespoons grated Parmesan cheese,
       divided
    1 cup (4 ounces) shredded mozzarella
       cheese
    1 cup thinly sliced onion
    7 to 9 plum tomatoes (about 1-1/4
       pounds), sliced
 1-1/2 teaspoons minced fresh oregano *or* 1/2
       teaspoon dried oregano
    1 teaspoon minced fresh thyme *or* 1/4
       teaspoon dried thyme
Salt and pepper to taste

Brush a 15-in. x 10-in. x 1-in. baking pan with some of the melted butter. Lay a sheet of phyllo in pan, folding edges in to fit (keep remaining dough covered with waxed paper to avoid drying out). Brush dough with butter and sprinkle with 1 tablespoon Parmesan cheese. Repeat layers five times, folding edges for each layer.

Top with remaining dough, folding edges to fit pan; brush with remaining butter. Sprinkle with mozzarella cheese; arrange onion and tomatoes over the cheese. Sprinkle with oregano, thyme, salt, pepper and remaining Parmesan. Bake at 375° for 20-25 minutes or until edges are golden brown. **Yield:** 28 slices.

Tomato Zucchini Stew

Tomato Zucchini Stew

(Pictured above)

This recipe's "famous" with my friends and the younger friends of my grown daughter and granddaughter. I make it for potlucks and other get-togethers.
—Helen Miller, Hickory Hills, Illinois

1-1/4 pounds bulk Italian sausage
1-1/2 cups sliced celery (3/4-inch pieces)
8 medium fresh tomatoes (about 4
   pounds), peeled and cut into sixths
1-1/2 cups tomato juice
   4 small zucchini, sliced into 1/4-inch
      pieces
2-1/2 teaspoons Italian seasoning
1-1/2 to 2 teaspoons salt
   1 teaspoon sugar
1/2 teaspoon garlic salt
1/2 teaspoon pepper
   3 cups canned *or* frozen corn
   2 medium green peppers, sliced
      into 1-inch pieces
1/4 cup cornstarch
1/4 cup water
Shredded mozzarella cheese

In a 4-qt. Dutch oven, cook sausage over medium heat until no longer pink. Add celery and cook for 15 minutes; drain. Add tomatoes, tomato juice, zucchini and seasonings; bring to a boil. Reduce heat; cover and simmer for 20 minutes. Add corn and peppers; cover and simmer for 15 minutes.

Combine cornstarch and water; stir into stew. Bring to a boil; cook and stir until mixture thickens. Sprinkle with cheese. **Yield:** 6-8 servings.

Editor's Note: Three 28-ounce cans of tomatoes with liquid (cut up) may be substituted for the fresh tomatoes and tomato juice.

Best-of-Show Tomato Quiche

I knew this delicious recipe was a "keeper" when I first tried it in the 1970s as a new bride—it impressed my in-laws when I made it for them! Now I sometimes substitute Mexican or Cajun seasoning for the basil. No matter how it's seasoned, it's wonderful.
—Dorothy Swanson, Affton, Missouri

3/4 cup all-purpose flour
1/2 cup cornmeal
1/2 teaspoon salt
1/8 teaspoon pepper
1/3 cup shortening
   4 to 5 tablespoons cold water
FILLING:
   2 cups chopped plum tomatoes
   1 teaspoon salt
1/2 teaspoon dried basil
1/8 teaspoon pepper
1/2 cup chopped green onions
1/2 cup shredded cheddar cheese
1/2 cup shredded Swiss cheese
   2 tablespoons all-purpose flour
   1 cup evaporated milk
   2 eggs

In a bowl, combine the first four ingredients. Cut in shortening until crumbly. Add water, tossing with a fork until the dough forms a ball. Refrigerate for 30 minutes.

On a lightly floured surface, roll out dough to fit a 9-in. pie plate; transfer pastry to plate. Trim to 1/2 in. beyond edge of plate; flute edges. Bake at 375° for 10 minutes. Cool completely.

Place tomatoes in the crust; sprinkle with salt, basil, pepper, onions and cheeses. In a bowl, whisk flour, milk and eggs until smooth. Pour over filling. Bake at 375° for 40-45 minutes or until a knife inserted near center comes out clean. Let stand for 10 minutes before cutting. **Yield:** 6-8 servings.

Smoked Salmon Cherry Tomatoes

These bright red festive bites are a showstopping finger food during the holiday season, at Easter and for the Fourth of July. With the smoked salmon filling,

these appetizers seem elegant…and they're convenient because you can prepare them ahead. —Pat Cronin
APO, Paris, France

30 cherry tomatoes
3 ounces smoked salmon, finely chopped
1/3 cup finely chopped onion
1/3 cup finely chopped green pepper
Salt and pepper to taste
1 package (3 ounces) cream cheese, softened
1 teaspoon milk
Fresh dill sprigs

Cut a thin slice off each tomato top. Scoop out; discard pulp. Invert tomatoes on paper towels to drain. In a bowl, combine salmon, onion, green pepper, salt and pepper; mix well. Spoon into tomatoes.

In a small mixing bowl, beat the cream cheese and milk until smooth. Insert a star tip into a pastry or plastic bag. Pipe a small amount of cream cheese mixture onto tomatoes. Garnish with dill. **Yield:** 2-1/2 dozen.

Bruschetta Chicken

I found the recipe years ago and have made this dish many times. It usually prompts recipe requests.
—Carolin Cattoi-Demkiw, Lethbridge, Alberta

✓ Uses less fat, sugar or salt. Includes Nutritional Analysis and Diabetic Exchanges.

1/2 cup all-purpose flour
2 eggs, lightly beaten
4 boneless skinless chicken breast halves (1 pound)
1/4 cup grated Parmesan cheese
1/4 cup dry bread crumbs
1 tablespoon butter, melted
2 large tomatoes, seeded and chopped
3 tablespoons minced fresh basil
2 garlic cloves, minced
1 tablespoon olive oil
1/2 teaspoon salt
1/4 teaspoon pepper

Place flour and eggs in separate shallow bowls. Dip chicken in flour, then in eggs; place in a greased 13-in. x 9-in. x 2-in. baking dish. Combine the Parmesan cheese, bread crumbs and butter; sprinkle over chicken. Loosely cover baking dish with foil. Bake at 375° for 20 minutes. Uncover; bake 5-10 minutes longer or until top is browned.

Meanwhile, in a bowl, combine the remaining ingredients. Spoon over the chicken. Return to the oven for 3-5 minutes or until tomato mixture is heated through. **Yield:** 4 servings.
Nutritional Analysis: One serving (prepared with 1/2 cup egg substitute) equals 358 calories, 13 g fat (5 g saturated fat), 86 mg cholesterol, 623 mg sodium, 22 g carbohydrate, 2 g fiber, 36 g protein. **Diabetic Exchanges:** 4-1/2 lean meat, 1 starch, 1 vegetable.

Spicy Tomato Juice

(Pictured below)

You can drink this juice plain or use it in most any recipe like chili that calls for vegetable juice as an ingredient. —Kathleen Gill, Butte, Montana

13 pounds ripe tomatoes (about 40 medium)
2 celery ribs, coarsely chopped
3 medium onions, coarsely chopped
1 medium green pepper, coarsely chopped
1-1/2 cups chopped fresh parsley
1/2 cup sugar
1 tablespoon Worcestershire sauce
4 teaspoons salt
1/4 teaspoon hot pepper sauce
1/4 teaspoon cayenne pepper
1/4 teaspoon pepper

Quarter tomatoes; place in a 6-qt. kettle. Add the celery, onions, green pepper and parsley. Simmer, uncovered, until vegetables are tender, about 45 minutes, stirring occasionally.

Cool slightly; put through a sieve or food mill. Return to kettle. Add remaining ingredients; mix well. Bring to a boil. Remove from the heat; cool. Pour into freezer containers, leaving 1/2-in. headspace. Freeze for up to 12 months. **Yield:** about 5 quarts.

Spicy Tomato Juice

Four-Tomato Salsa

(Pictured below)

A variety of tomatoes, onions and peppers makes this chunky salsa so good. Whenever I try to take a batch to a get-together, it's hard to keep my family from finishing it off first! —Connie Siese, Wayne, Michigan

 Uses less fat, sugar or salt. Includes Nutritional Analysis and Diabetic Exchanges.

> 7 plum tomatoes, chopped
> 7 medium tomatoes, chopped
> 3 medium yellow tomatoes, chopped
> 3 medium orange tomatoes, chopped
> 1 teaspoon salt
> 2 tablespoons lime juice
> 2 tablespoons olive oil
> 1 medium white onion, chopped
> 2/3 cup chopped red onion
> 2 green onions, chopped
> 1/2 cup *each* chopped sweet red, orange, yellow and green pepper
> 3 pepperoncinis, chopped
> 3 pickled sweet banana wax peppers, chopped
> 1/2 cup minced fresh parsley
> 2 tablespoons minced fresh cilantro
> 1 tablespoon dried chervil

Tortilla chips

In a colander, combine the tomatoes and salt. Let drain for 10 minutes. Transfer to a large bowl. Stir in the lime juice, oil, onions, peppers, parsley, cilantro and chervil. Serve with tortilla chips. Refrigerate or freeze leftovers. **Yield:** 14 cups.

Nutritional Analysis: One serving (1/4 cup salsa) equals 16 calories, 1 g fat (0 saturated fat), 0 cholesterol, 63 mg sodium, 3 g carbohydrate, 1 g fiber, 1 g protein. **Diabetic Exchange:** Free food.

Editor's Note: Look for pepperoncinis (pickled peppers) and pickled banana peppers in the pickle and olive aisle of your grocery store. When cutting or seeding hot peppers, use plastic or rubber gloves to protect your hands. Avoid touching your face.

Four-Tomato Salsa

Chunky Ketchup

I came up with this chunky homemade ketchup to jazz up chopped steak sandwiches and hot sausage sandwiches for my family. I gave some to friends, and they enjoyed it on hamburgers and stuffed peppers. —Susan Stahr, Driftwood, Pennsylvania

> 8 cups chopped seeded peeled tomatoes
> 2 medium onions, chopped
> 2 medium green peppers, chopped
> 2 cups sugar
> 2 cans (6 ounces *each*) tomato paste
> 2 tablespoons salt
> 1/2 cup white vinegar

In a large saucepan, combine the tomatoes, onions, green peppers, sugar, tomato paste and salt; bring to a boil. Reduce heat; simmer, uncovered, for 1-1/2 hours or until slightly thickened.

Stir in vinegar; heat through. Ladle hot mixture into hot jars, leaving 1/4-in. headspace. Adjust caps. Process for 20 minutes in a boiling-water bath. **Yield:** 3-1/2 pints.

Italian Pasta Salad

This zesty recipe combines vegetables and pasta in a creamy dressing. Refreshing and filling, this change-of-pace salad is perfect as a side dish. It's always popular at a potluck. —Tina Dierking, Canaan, Maine

> 3/4 cup uncooked spiral pasta
> 1-1/2 cups halved cherry tomatoes
> 1 cup sliced fresh mushrooms
> 1/4 cup chopped sweet red pepper
> 1/4 cup chopped green pepper
> 3 tablespoons thinly sliced green onions
> 1-1/2 cups zesty Italian salad dressing
> 3/4 cup mayonnaise
> 1/2 cup grated Parmesan cheese
> 1/3 cup cubed provolone cheese
> 1 can (2-1/4 ounces) sliced ripe olives, drained

Leaf lettuce, optional

Cook pasta according to package directions; rinse with cold water and drain. Place in a bowl; add the tomatoes, mushrooms, peppers, onions and salad dressing. Cover and refrigerate for at least 4 hours or overnight; drain.

In a bowl, combine the mayonnaise and Parme-

san cheese; stir in the provolone cheese and olives. Gently fold into the pasta mixture. Serve in a lettuce-lined bowl if desired. **Yield:** 6 servings.

BLT Brunch Pie

My boys can't wait to pick the first ripe tomatoes in our garden to be used in this terrific pie. It has a tempting filling and tomatoes layered in a melt-in-your-mouth crust. And the crust is so easy to make—you just pat the dough into the pan! —Shara Walvoort
Oostburg, Wisconsin

1-1/4 cups all-purpose flour
   2 teaspoons baking powder
   1/2 teaspoon salt
   1/2 teaspoon dried basil
   1/2 cup shortening
   1/2 cup sour cream
FILLING:
   3/4 cup mayonnaise
   1 cup (4 ounces) shredded cheddar cheese
   1 can (4-1/2 ounces) mushroom stems and pieces, drained
   8 bacon strips, cooked and crumbled
   1 tablespoon chopped green pepper
   1 tablespoon chopped onion
   3 medium tomatoes, peeled and sliced

In a bowl, combine the first four ingredients. Cut in shortening until crumbly. Stir in sour cream. Cover and refrigerate for 30 minutes. Press pastry into a 9-in. pie plate; flute edges if desired. Bake at 375°

for 10 minutes. Cool completely.

In a bowl, combine the mayonnaise, cheese, mushrooms, bacon, green pepper and onion. Layer half of the tomatoes in crust; top with half of the mayonnaise mixture. Repeat layers. Bake at 350° for 30-35 minutes or until golden brown. Refrigerate leftovers. **Yield:** 6-8 servings.

Editor's Note: Reduced-fat or fat-free sour cream and mayonnaise may not be substituted for regular sour cream and mayonnaise.

Tomatoes and Cukes

(Pictured above)

Sometimes, simple is best. That's how I feel about this quick and refreshing summertime salad—a delightful dressing lets the garden-fresh vegetables star. It takes only a few minutes to arrange the slices attractively on a bed of lettuce. —Dorothy Bateman
Carver, Massachusetts

   2 tablespoons olive oil
   1 tablespoon vinegar
   1 tablespoon minced fresh parsley
   1/4 teaspoon salt
   1/4 teaspoon pepper
   3 medium tomatoes, sliced
   1/2 large cucumber, sliced
Leaf lettuce, optional

In a small bowl, whisk oil, vinegar, parsley, salt and pepper. On a serving plate, arrange tomato and cucumber slices over lettuce if desired. Drizzle with the vinaigrette. **Yield:** 4 servings.

49

Broccoli Orange Salad
Wild Rice Floret Bake
Cream of Cauliflower Soup
Bacon-Broccoli Cheese Ball

Chapter 7
Broccoli & Cauliflower

Bacon-Broccoli Cheese Ball

(Pictured at left)

Needing a quick appetizer one night when dinner was running late, I combined a few leftovers into this easy cheese ball. For variety, you can shape it into a log, or substitute your favorite herbs for the pepper.
—Tamara Rickard, Bartlett, Tennessee

- 1 package (8 ounces) cream cheese, softened
- 1 cup (4 ounces) finely shredded cheddar cheese
- 1/2 teaspoon pepper
- 1 cup finely chopped broccoli florets
- 6 bacon strips, cooked and crumbled

Assorted crackers

In a mixing bowl, beat cream cheese, cheddar cheese and pepper until blended. Stir in broccoli. Shape into a ball and roll in bacon. Cover and refrigerate. Remove from the refrigerator 15 minutes before serving. Serve with crackers. **Yield:** 2-1/2 cups.

Cream of Cauliflower Soup

(Pictured at left)

I adapted this rich and creamy concoction from a recipe I tasted at a local restaurant...and it's since become a popular item on my "menu". It's so much better than the canned variety. *—Carol Reaves*
San Antonio, Texas

- 2 medium onions, chopped
- 2 medium carrots, grated
- 2 celery ribs, sliced
- 2 garlic cloves, minced
- 1/4 cup plus 6 tablespoons butter, *divided*
- 1 medium head cauliflower, chopped
- 5 cups chicken broth
- 1/4 cup minced fresh parsley
- 1 teaspoon salt
- 1 teaspoon coarsely ground pepper
- 1/2 teaspoon dried basil
- 1/2 teaspoon dried tarragon
- 6 tablespoons all-purpose flour
- 1 cup milk
- 1/2 cup heavy whipping cream
- 1/4 cup sour cream

Fresh tarragon, optional

In a soup kettle or Dutch oven, saute the onions, carrots, celery and garlic in 1/4 cup butter until tender. Add cauliflower, broth, parsley, salt, pepper, basil and tarragon. Cover and simmer for 30 minutes or until the vegetables are tender.

Meanwhile, in a saucepan, melt the remaining butter. Stir in flour until smooth. Gradually stir in the milk and whipping cream. Bring to a boil; cook and stir for 2 minutes or until thickened. Add to cauliflower mixture. Cook for 10 minutes or until thickened, stirring frequently. Remove from the heat; stir in sour cream. Garnish with tarragon if desired. **Yield:** 8 servings.

Floret Hints

I buy a large amount of fresh broccoli, wash it, blanch it in boiling water for a couple minutes and freeze in freezer bags. It always tastes garden-fresh. *—Tamra Harrington*
Scottsdale, Arizona

To help cauliflower retain its color while cooking, add a small amount of nonfat dry milk to the cooking water. *—Catherine Funk*
Andover, Minnesota

Chicken Broccoli Casserole

Chicken Broccoli Casserole

(Pictured above)

Broccoli is a favorite vegetable in our home. This dish featuring that veggie always get raves. —Colleen Lewis Cottonwood, Arizona

> 3 cups broccoli florets (about 1-1/4 pounds)
> 2 cups cubed cooked chicken *or* turkey
> 1 can (10-3/4 ounces) condensed cream of chicken soup, undiluted
> 1/2 cup mayonnaise
> 1/2 cup grated Parmesan cheese
> 1/2 teaspoon curry powder
> 1 cup cubed fresh bread
> 2 tablespoons butter, melted

In a covered saucepan, cook the broccoli in water until crisp-tender; drain. Place in a greased 11-in. x 7-in. x 2-in. baking dish; set aside. Combine the chicken, soup, mayonnaise, Parmesan cheese and curry powder; spoon over the broccoli. Top with bread cubes and butter. Bake, uncovered, at 350° for 25-30 minutes or until heated through. **Yield:** 6 servings.

Wild Rice Floret Bake

(Pictured on page 50)

My mom used to make this hearty dish for family get-togethers. Now I do the same. Calling for both cooked broccoli and cauliflower, this crowd-pleasing casserole is doubly delicious. —Donna Torgerson Park Rapids, Minnesota

> 1 medium onion, chopped
> 3 tablespoons butter
> 2 tablespoons all-purpose flour
> 1/2 teaspoon salt
> Dash pepper
> 2 cups milk
> 1 cup (8 ounces) sour cream
> 1 cup (4 ounces) shredded cheddar cheese, *divided*
> 4 cups cooked wild rice, *divided*
> 6 cups chopped cooked broccoli (about 1 large bunch)
> 5 cups chopped cooked cauliflower (about 1 small head)
> 6 bacon strips, cooked and crumbled

In a saucepan, saute the onion in butter until tender. Stir in flour, salt and pepper until blended. Gradually add milk. Bring to a boil; cook and stir for 2 minutes or until thickened and bubbly. Remove from the heat; stir in sour cream and 1/2 cup cheese until smooth.

Place 2 cups wild rice in a greased 13-in. x 9-in. x 2-in. baking dish. Top with broccoli and cauliflower. Place remaining wild rice lengthwise down the center of dish. Pour the sauce over all. Sprinkle with remaining cheese. Cover and bake at 350° for 20 minutes. Uncover; sprinkle with bacon. Bake 10-15 minutes longer or until bubbly. **Yield:** 8-10 servings.

Broccoli Orange Salad

(Pictured on page 50)

Every time I take this sweet orangy salad to a potluck, I pass around the recipe right away, too, since people always ask for it. It's popular at all sorts of gatherings. —Cathy Lavers, Scotsburn, Nova Scotia

> 1 egg
> 1/4 cup sugar
> 1-1/2 teaspoons honey
> 1 teaspoon ground mustard
> 1/2 teaspoon cornstarch
> 2 tablespoons water
> 2 tablespoons white wine vinegar
> 2 tablespoons mayonnaise
> 2 tablespoons sour cream
> 4-1/2 teaspoons butter
> 4 cups broccoli florets (about 1 medium bunch)
> 1 cup salted cashews
> 1 cup cubed Swiss cheese
> 1 can (11 ounces) mandarin oranges, well drained
> 1/2 cup raisins
> 6 bacon strips, cooked and crumbled
> 1/2 cup chopped red onion, optional

In a heavy saucepan, combine egg, sugar, honey, mustard and cornstarch with a whisk until smooth. Gradually whisk in water and vinegar. Cook and stir over medium heat until a thermometer reads 160° and mixture is thickened. Remove from the heat; stir in mayonnaise, sour cream and butter until blended. Cool.

Meanwhile, in a large bowl, combine broccoli, cashews, cheese, oranges, raisins, bacon and onion if desired. Just before serving, add dressing and toss to coat. **Yield:** 8-10 servings.

End of Summer Vegetable Bake

When my husband worked as a deputy ag commissioner, he'd bring me bushels of vegetables from area farms. This pretty side dish is the result. It's easy to fix but impressive enough for company.
—Judy Williams, Hayden, Idaho

    1 small head cauliflower, broken into
       small florets (about 5 cups)
    1 medium bunch broccoli, cut into small
       florets (about 4 cups)
    1 medium onion, chopped
    2 garlic cloves, minced
    1 tablespoon butter
    2 medium tomatoes, chopped
  3/4 teaspoon dried basil
  3/4 teaspoon dried oregano
  3/4 teaspoon salt
  1/4 teaspoon pepper
  1/4 teaspoon hot pepper sauce
    4 eggs
  1/3 cup half-and-half cream
1-1/2 cups (6 ounces) shredded Swiss
       cheese, *divided*
  1/4 cup shredded Parmesan cheese

Place the cauliflower and broccoli in a saucepan with a small amount of water. Bring to a boil. Reduce heat; cover and simmer for 5-10 minutes or until crisp-tender. Drain and set aside.

In a large skillet, saute onion and garlic in butter until tender. Stir in tomatoes, seasonings, cauliflower and broccoli. Cook, uncovered, until heated through, about 4 minutes, stirring occasionally. Remove from the heat and set aside.

In a large bowl, beat eggs and cream; stir in 1 cup Swiss cheese, Parmesan cheese and the vegetable mixture. Transfer to a greased shallow 2-qt. baking dish. Sprinkle with remaining Swiss cheese. Bake, uncovered, at 375° for 25-30 min-

utes or until a knife inserted near the center comes out clean. Let stand 10 minutes before serving. **Yield:** 12 servings.

Picante Broccoli Chicken Salad

(Pictured below)

Since our family likes things spicy, I often add a fresh jalapeno pepper to this salad. It's a simple, savory way to use up leftover chicken. Plus, it's so eye-catching, it could double as the main dish and the table centerpiece!
—Krista Shumway, Billings, Montana

  1/2 cup mayonnaise
  1/4 cup picante sauce
    1 garlic clove, minced
  1/2 to 1 teaspoon chili powder
    2 cups cubed cooked chicken
    2 cups broccoli florets
    1 cup diced fresh tomato
  1/2 cup shredded cheddar cheese
  1/2 cup chopped onion
  1/4 cup julienned green pepper
  1/4 cup julienned sweet red pepper
Flour tortillas, warmed

In a large bowl, combine the first four ingredients; mix well. Add chicken, broccoli, tomato, cheese, onion and peppers; toss to coat. Refrigerate for at least 30 minutes before serving. Serve with tortillas. **Yield:** 6-8 servings.

Picante Broccoli Chicken Salad

Broccoli Fish Bundles

(Pictured below)

These bundles take a little time to assemble, but they're worth it! They're always popular at a shower or buffet...and they're great for an everyday dinner, too.
—*Frances Quinn, Farmingdale, New York*

- 18 fresh broccoli spears (about 1-1/2 pounds)
- 6 cubes Monterey Jack cheese (1-1/2 inches)
- 6 sole *or* flounder fillets (about 2 pounds)
- 1/8 teaspoon lemon-pepper seasoning, optional
- 1/3 cup butter, melted
- 2 teaspoons lemon juice
- 1 garlic clove, minced
- 1/4 teaspoon salt
- 1/8 teaspoon pepper

In a saucepan, place broccoli in a small amount of water. Bring to a boil. Reduce heat; cover and simmer for 2-3 minutes or until crisp-tender. Rinse in cold water; drain.

For each bundle, place a cheese cube on three broccoli spears. Wrap with a fish fillet and fasten with a toothpick if necessary. Place on a greased foil-lined baking sheet. Sprinkle with lemon-pepper if desired. Bake at 350° for 15-25 minutes or until fish flakes easily with a fork.

Meanwhile, combine butter, lemon juice, garlic, salt and pepper. Transfer fish bundles to a serving platter; remove toothpicks. Drizzle with butter mixture. **Yield:** 6 servings.

Broccoli Fish Bundles

Savory Cauliflower Pie

If you're looking for a meatless main dish or a hearty side to take to a church potluck or family gathering, try this pie.
—*Debbie Hart, Ft. Wayne, Indiana*

- 3 cups seasoned croutons, crushed
- 1/2 cup butter, melted, *divided*
- 1 small head cauliflower, cut into small florets (about 5 cups)
- 1 cup chopped onion
- 1/2 cup thinly sliced carrot
- 1 garlic clove, minced
- 1/2 teaspoon salt
- 1/4 to 1/2 teaspoon dried oregano
- 1 cup (4 ounces) shredded cheddar cheese, *divided*
- 2 eggs
- 1/4 cup milk

In a bowl, combine croutons and 1/4 cup butter. Press onto the bottom and up the sides of an ungreased 9-in. pie plate. Bake at 375° for 8 minutes or until lightly browned; set aside.

In a large skillet, saute the cauliflower, onion, carrot, garlic, salt and oregano in remaining butter over medium heat for 10 minutes, stirring frequently. Sprinkle 1/2 cup cheese into prepared crust. Top with the cauliflower mixture and remaining cheese. In a bowl, beat the eggs and milk. Pour over pie.

Bake, uncovered, at 375° for 30 minutes or until a knife inserted near center comes out clean and cauliflower is tender. **Yield:** 6-8 servings.

Broccoli Cauliflower Salad

This salad has been to as many family gatherings as I have! It holds well and leftovers are tasty a day later.
—*Linda Kangas, Outlook, Saskatchewan*

- 1 medium head cauliflower, broken into florets (about 7-1/2 cups)
- 1 medium bunch broccoli, cut into florets (about 4 cups)
- 2 cups seedless red grapes
- 6 green onions with tops, sliced
- 2 cups (8 ounces) shredded mozzarella cheese
- 2 cups mayonnaise
- 1/4 cup grated Parmesan cheese
- 2 tablespoons sugar
- 2 tablespoons vinegar
- 1/2 to 1 pound sliced bacon, cooked and crumbled

Leaf lettuce

In a large bowl, combine the cauliflower, broccoli, grapes, onions and mozzarella cheese. Combine the mayonnaise, Parmesan cheese, sugar and vinegar; pour over vegetable mixture and toss to coat. Cover and refrigerate for at least 2 hours.

Just before serving, stir in bacon. Transfer to a lettuce-lined bowl. **Yield:** 15-20 servings.

Cauliflower Spinach Salad

Cauliflower, mandarin oranges, green pepper and radishes flavorfully dress up plain fresh spinach in this quick and easy salad.
—Marjorie Carey
Freeport, Florida

    2 cups cauliflowerets
    1 can (11 ounces) mandarin oranges, well
       drained
1/4 cup chopped green pepper
    2 large radishes, sliced
    4 cups torn fresh spinach
    1 can (5 ounces) evaporated milk
1/3 cup orange juice concentrate

In a large bowl, combine the first five ingredients. Pour milk in a small bowl; gradually whisk in orange juice concentrate. Drizzle over salad and toss to coat. Refrigerate leftovers. **Yield:** 8-10 servings.

Broccoli Soup

This thick creamy soup has wonderful broccoli flavor with just a hint of nutmeg. It's delicious!
—Marion Tipton, Phoenix, Arizona

    4 cups chicken broth
    2 to 2-1/2 pounds broccoli, cut into florets
1/2 cup chopped green onions
    1 tablespoon olive oil
1/4 cup all-purpose flour
    1 teaspoon salt
1/4 teaspoon ground nutmeg
1/8 teaspoon pepper
    1 cup half-and-half cream

In a large saucepan, bring the broth to a boil; add broccoli. Reduce heat; cover and simmer until tender, about 10 minutes. Meanwhile, in a small skillet, saute onions in oil until tender; stir into broth. Remove from the heat; cool 10-15 minutes. Puree in small batches in a blender or food processor until smooth. Return all to the saucepan; set aside.

In a bowl, combine flour, salt, nutmeg and pepper. Slowly add cream, stirring constantly. Gradually stir into broccoli mixture. Return to the heat; cook over medium until heated through, stirring occasionally. **Yield:** 4 servings.

Breaded Cauliflower

Breaded Cauliflower

(Pictured above)

My mother gets the credit for this delicious dish, which is a mainstay at our house. It can be an appetizer or side dish.
—Sandra Furman-Krajewski
Amsterdam, New York

    1 small head cauliflower, broken into
       florets (about 5 cups)
    4 egg yolks
    1 teaspoon garlic powder
    1 teaspoon onion powder
    1 teaspoon minced fresh parsley
1/2 teaspoon sugar
1/2 teaspoon salt
1/4 teaspoon pepper
    1 cup seasoned bread crumbs
    3 tablespoons grated Parmesan cheese
3/4 cup butter
Minced fresh parsley, optional

Place cauliflower and a small amount of water in a skillet. Bring to a boil. Reduce heat; cover and simmer until crisp-tender, about 8 minutes. Drain and set aside.

In a bowl, whisk egg yolks and seasonings. Place bread crumbs and Parmesan cheese in a large resealable plastic bag. Add a few florets at a time to the egg mixture; toss to coat. Using a slotted spoon, transfer cauliflower to crumb mixture; toss to coat.

In a skillet, melt the butter over medium-high heat. Cook cauliflower in batches until golden brown, about 4 minutes. Sprinkle with parsley if desired. **Yield:** 4-6 servings.

Fresh Corn Salad
Pork Chops with Corn Dressing
Corn Balls
Corn and Sausage Chowder

Chapter 8
Corn

Corn Balls

(Pictured at left)

Whenever I serve my Corn Balls, it's just about certain someone will ask for the recipe—I've gotten more requests for it than any other I've ever tried. I usually make them when we have company as a nice change-of-pace side dish. They're great with ham, steak or roast beef.
—Sharon Knicely
Harrisonburg, Virginia

1/2 cup chopped onion
1 cup chopped celery
1/2 cup butter
3-1/2 cups herb-seasoned stuffing croutons
3 cups cooked whole kernel corn
3 eggs, beaten
1/2 cup water
1/2 teaspoon salt
1/4 teaspoon pepper

In a saucepan, cook onion and celery in butter until tender; set aside to cool. In a bowl, combine croutons, corn, eggs, water, salt, pepper and onion mixture; mix well. Shape into eight to 10 balls. Place in an ungreased shallow baking dish. Bake, uncovered, at 375° for 25-30 minutes. **Yield:** 8-10 servings.

Pork Chops with Corn Dressing

(Pictured at left)

As a new bride, I came across the original version of this recipe in a newspaper. I changed it around some and tried it out on my groom. It became a family favorite—not to mention a great easy main course for unexpected company!
—June Hassler
Sultan, Washington

1 egg, beaten
2 cups soft bread crumbs

1-1/2 cups cooked whole kernel corn *or* 1 can
(17 ounces) whole kernel corn, drained
1/4 cup water
1/2 cup chopped green pepper
1 small onion, chopped
1 teaspoon Worcestershire sauce
2 tablespoons vegetable oil
6 butterfly-cut boneless pork loin chops
(about 1 inch thick)
Salt and pepper to taste
1 can (10-3/4 ounces) condensed cream of
mushroom soup, undiluted
2/3 cup milk

In a bowl, combine egg, bread crumbs, corn, water, green pepper, onion and Worcestershire sauce; set aside. In a large ovenproof skillet or a Dutch oven, heat oil over medium-high. Lightly brown pork chops on both sides. Season with salt and pepper.

Top with corn dressing mixture. Add enough water to cover bottom of pan. Bake, uncovered, at 350° for about 1 hour or until pork is tender. Add additional water to pan if necessary.

Remove pork chops and dressing to a serving platter and keep warm. Add the soup and milk to the pan drippings. Cook and stir over medium heat until hot and bubbly. Serve with the pork chops. **Yield:** 6 servings.

Corn Kernels

On ripe ears of corn, the silks are brown and dried on the ends. Peel down the husk and poke your thumb into a kernel. Look for clear juice to squirt out. The more milky the juice, the older and more starchy the corn.
—Janice Arnold, Gansevoort, New York

For a sweet treat, make herb butter to spread on corn on the cob. Combine 2 sticks of softened butter with 1 teaspoon chopped fresh basil or 1/2 teaspoon dried basil.
—Ellen Bower, Taneytown, Maryland

Fresh Corn Cakes

Fresh Corn Cakes

(Pictured above)

Corn's always been the basis of my best recipes—these corn cakes are a favorite. For dinner, they're nice with fresh fruit salad and ham. They're also great with breakfast sausage and orange juice. —Gaynelle Fritsch
Welches, Oregon

  1 cup all-purpose flour
1/2 cup yellow *or* blue cornmeal
  1 tablespoon sugar
  1 tablespoon baking powder
1/2 teaspoon salt
  2 eggs, *separated*
  1 cup milk
1/4 cup butter, melted
  1 cup cooked whole kernel corn
  4 green onions, thinly sliced
1/2 medium sweet red pepper, finely
     chopped
  1 can (4 ounces) chopped green chilies
Butter *or* vegetable oil for frying
Maple syrup, optional

In a medium bowl, combine flour, cornmeal, sugar, baking powder and salt. In a small bowl, beat egg yolks; blend in milk and butter. Add to dry ingredients; stir until just mixed. (Batter may be slightly lumpy). Stir in the corn, green onions, red pepper and green chilies; set aside. In a small mixing bowl, beat egg whites until stiff peaks form. Gently fold into batter.

For each pancake, pour about 1/4 cup batter onto a lightly greased hot griddle; turn when bubbles form on tops of cakes. Cook second side until golden brown. Serve immediately with syrup if desired. **Yield:** 20 pancakes.

Fresh Corn Salad

(Pictured on page 56)

People who prefer food with some tang find this corn salad particularly appealing. —Carol Shaffer
Cape Girardeau, Missouri

 Uses less fat, sugar or salt. Includes Nutritional Analysis and Diabetic Exchanges.

  8 ears fresh corn, husked and cleaned
1/2 cup vegetable oil
1/4 cup cider vinegar
1-1/2 teaspoons lemon juice
1/4 cup minced fresh parsley
  2 teaspoons sugar
  1 teaspoon salt, optional
1/2 teaspoon dried basil
1/8 to 1/4 teaspoon cayenne pepper
  2 large tomatoes, seeded and coarsely
     chopped
1/2 cup chopped onion
1/3 cup chopped green pepper
1/3 cup chopped sweet red pepper

In a large saucepan, cook corn in enough boiling water to cover for 5-7 minutes or until tender. Drain, cool and set aside. In a large bowl, mix the oil, vinegar, lemon juice, parsley, sugar, salt if desired, basil and cayenne pepper.

Cut cooled corn off the cob (should measure 4 cups). Add corn, tomatoes, onion and peppers to the oil mixture. Mix well. Cover and chill for several hours or overnight. **Yield:** 10 servings.

Nutritional Analysis: One serving (without added salt) equals 102 calories, 251 mg sodium, 0 cholesterol, 21 g carbohydrate, 3 g protein, 2 g fat. **Diabetic Exchanges:** 1 starch, 1/2 vegetable, 1/2 fat.

Corn and Sausage Chowder

(Pictured on page 56)

I've had several cooking "teachers" over the years—my Irish grandmother...my mother...and the restaurant my husband and I operated in Manitoba at one time!
—Joanne Watts, Kitchener, Ontario

  3 ears fresh corn, husked and cleaned
  4 cups heavy whipping cream
  2 cups chicken broth
  4 garlic cloves, minced
 10 fresh thyme sprigs
  1 bay leaf
1-1/2 medium onions, finely chopped, *divided*

1/2 pound hot Italian sausage links
2 tablespoons butter
2 teaspoons minced jalapeno peppers
  with seeds
1/2 teaspoon ground cumin
2 tablespoons all-purpose flour
2 medium potatoes, peeled and cut
  into 1/2-inch cubes
Salt and pepper to taste
1-1/2 teaspoons snipped fresh chives

Using a small sharp knife, cut corn from cobs; set corn aside. Place the corncobs, cream, broth, garlic, thyme, bay leaf and one-third of the onions in a large saucepan. Heat almost to boiling; reduce heat and simmer, covered, for 1 hour, stirring occasionally. Remove and discard corncobs. Strain cream mixture through a sieve set over a large bowl, pressing solids with back of spoon; set aside.

Meanwhile, brown sausage in a large skillet. Cool and cut into 1/2-in. slices. In a large saucepan, melt butter. Add jalapenos, cumin and remaining onions; cook 5 minutes. Stir in flour; cook and stir 2 minutes. Gradually add corn stock. Add sausage and potatoes. Cover and cook until potatoes are tender, about 25 minutes. Add corn and cook just until tender, about 5 minutes.

Remove bay leaf. Season with salt and pepper. For a thinner chowder, add additional chicken broth. Sprinkle with chives before serving. **Yield:** 8 servings (2 quarts).

Editor's Note: When cutting or seeding hot peppers, use plastic or rubber gloves to protect your hands. Avoid touching your face.

Delicious Corn Pudding

This comforting dish was part of family meals for years and shared at gatherings. —Paula Marchesi
Rocky Point, New York

4 eggs, *separated*
2 tablespoons butter, melted and cooled
1 tablespoon sugar
1 tablespoon brown sugar
1 teaspoon salt
1/2 teaspoon vanilla extract
Pinch ground cinnamon and nutmeg
2 cups fresh whole kernel corn
1 cup half-and-half cream
1 cup milk

In a mixing bowl, beat egg yolks until thick and lemon-colored, about 5-8 minutes. Add butter, sugars, salt, vanilla, cinnamon and nutmeg; mix well. Add corn. Stir in cream and milk. Beat egg whites until stiff; fold into yolk mixture.

Pour into a greased 1-1/2-qt. baking dish. Bake, uncovered, at 350° for 35 minutes or until a knife

inserted near the center comes out clean. Cover loosely during last 10 minutes of baking if necessary to prevent overbrowning. **Yield:** 8 servings.

Corn and Chicken Dinner

(Pictured below)

My interests are reading, gardening...and growing most of the ingredients I use in this dinner! There's something for every taste in this recipe.
—Doralee Pinkerton, Milford, Indiana

3 garlic cloves, minced, *divided*
1/2 cup butter, *divided*
3 pounds chicken legs and thighs
  (about 8 pieces)
3 ears fresh corn, husked, cleaned and cut
  into thirds
1/4 cup water
2 teaspoons dried tarragon, *divided*
1/2 teaspoon salt
1/4 teaspoon pepper
2 medium zucchini, sliced into 1/2-inch
  pieces
2 tomatoes, seeded and cut into chunks

In a Dutch oven or large skillet over medium-high heat, saute 2 of the garlic cloves in 2 tablespoons butter. Add the chicken and brown on both sides. Reduce heat. Add corn and water. Sprinkle with 1 teaspoon tarragon, salt and pepper. Cover and simmer for 20-25 minutes or until chicken is tender.

Meanwhile, in a small saucepan, melt remaining butter. Add remaining garlic and tarragon; simmer for 3 minutes. Layer zucchini and tomatoes over chicken mixture. Drizzle seasoned butter over all; cover and cook for 3-5 minutes. **Yield:** 6-8 servings.

Corn and Chicken Dinner

Colossal Cornburger

(Pictured below)

It's been such a long time since I added this recipe to my file that I don't even remember where it came from. Cooking's something I thoroughly enjoy—and, when I'm finished, my husband always wonders which truck ran through our kitchen!
—Lesley Colgan
London, Ontario

  1 egg, beaten
  1 cup cooked whole kernel corn
1/2 cup coarsely crushed cheese crackers
1/4 cup sliced green onions
1/4 cup chopped fresh parsley
  1 teaspoon Worcestershire sauce
  2 pounds ground beef
  1 teaspoon salt
1/2 teaspoon pepper
1/2 teaspoon rubbed sage

In a medium bowl, combine egg, corn, crackers, green onions, parsley and Worcestershire sauce; set aside. In a large bowl, combine ground beef and seasonings.

On sheets of waxed paper, pat half of the beef mixture at a time into an 8-1/2-in. circle. Spoon corn mixture onto one circle of meat to within 1 in. of the edge. Top with second circle of meat; remove top sheet of waxed paper and seal edges. Invert onto a well-greased wire grill basket; peel off waxed paper. Grill over medium heat, turning once, for 25-30 minutes or until meat is no longer pink.

For oven method, place burger on a baking pan.

Colossal Cornburger

Bake at 350° for 40-45 minutes or until meat is no longer pink. Cut into wedges to serve. **Yield:** 6 servings.

Corn Tortilla Pizzas

These tasty individual pizzas have the zippy flavor of tacos. When I created this recipe and served these pizzas to my husband and day-care kids, they made them disappear. The recipe produces a big batch of the meat mixture, but leftovers can be frozen for up to 3 months.
—Karen Housley-Raatz
Walworth, Wisconsin

1-1/4 pounds ground beef
  1 small onion, chopped
1/2 cup chopped green pepper
  3 cans (6 ounces *each*) tomato paste
1-1/4 cups water
  1 cup salsa
  2 cups fresh *or* frozen corn
1-1/2 cups chopped fresh tomatoes
3/4 cup chopped ripe olives
  1 envelope taco seasoning
  3 teaspoons garlic powder
1-1/2 teaspoons dried parsley flakes
1/2 teaspoon dried oregano
1/8 teaspoon salt
1/4 teaspoon pepper
 32 corn *or* flour tortillas (6 inches)
  8 cups (2 pounds) shredded mozzarella cheese

In a skillet over medium heat, cook beef, onion and green pepper until meat is no longer pink; drain. In a bowl, combine tomato paste and water until blended; add salsa. Stir into meat mixture. Stir in the corn, tomatoes, olives and seasonings.

Place tortillas on ungreased baking sheets. Spread each with 1/4 cup meat mixture to within 1/2 in. of edge and sprinkle with 1/4 cup of cheese. Bake at 375° for 5-7 minutes or until the cheese is melted. **Yield:** 32 pizzas.

Corny Tomato Dumpling Soup

I have a big garden on our farm and enjoy cooking with my harvest. In this savory tomato soup, corn stars in both the broth and dumplings. It has a fresh-picked flavor. Ground beef makes it a hearty first course or satisfying light main dish.
—Jackie Ferris
Tiverton, Ontario

  1 pound ground beef
  3 cups fresh *or* frozen corn
  1 can (28 ounces) diced tomatoes, undrained

2 cans (14-1/2 ounces *each*) beef broth
1 cup chopped onion
1 garlic clove, minced
1-1/2 teaspoons dried basil
1-1/2 teaspoons dried thyme
1/2 teaspoon dried rosemary, crushed
Salt and pepper to taste
CORN DUMPLINGS:
1 cup all-purpose flour
1/2 cup cornmeal
2-1/2 teaspoons baking powder
1/2 teaspoon salt
1 egg
2/3 cup milk
1 cup fresh *or* frozen corn
1/2 cup shredded cheddar cheese
1 tablespoon minced fresh parsley

In a large saucepan or Dutch oven over medium heat, cook beef until no longer pink; drain. Stir in corn, tomatoes, broth, onion, garlic and seasonings. Bring to a boil. Reduce heat; cover and simmer for 30-45 minutes.

For dumplings, combine flour, cornmeal, baking powder and salt in a bowl. In another bowl, beat egg; stir in milk, corn, cheese and parsley. Stir into dry ingredients just until moistened. Drop by tablespoonfuls onto simmering soup. Cover and simmer for 15 minutes or until a toothpick inserted in a dumpling comes out clean (do not lift cover while simmering). **Yield:** 8 servings (about 2 quarts).

Romaine Roasted Corn

Amaze your family and friends with this fun and different way to cook corn on the cob. Wrapped in lettuce and baked, the corn is tender and delicious...and the ears stay nicely coated with tasty herb butter.
—Margaret Wagner Allen, Abingdon, Virginia

6 tablespoons butter, softened
1 teaspoon dried rosemary, crushed
1/2 teaspoon dried marjoram
6 ears corn on the cob, husks removed
1 bunch romaine
Salt and pepper to taste

In a mixing bowl, combine the butter, rosemary and marjoram; spread over corn. Wrap each ear in two to three romaine leaves. Place in a 13-in. x 9-in. x 2-in. baking dish. Cover and bake at 450° for 30-35 minutes or until corn is tender. Discard romaine before serving. Sprinkle corn with salt and pepper. **Yield:** 6 servings.

Egg and Corn Quesadilla

Egg and Corn Quesadilla

(Pictured above)

For a deliciously different breakfast or brunch, try this excellent quesadilla. It's also great for a light lunch or supper. Corn is a natural in Southwestern cooking.
—Stacy Joura, Stoneboro, Pennsylvania

1 medium onion, chopped
1 medium green pepper, chopped
1 garlic clove, minced
2 tablespoons olive oil
3 cups fresh *or* frozen corn
1 teaspoon minced chives
1/2 teaspoon dried cilantro flakes
1/2 teaspoon salt
1/4 teaspoon pepper
4 eggs, beaten
4 flour tortillas (10 inches)
1/2 cup salsa
1 cup (8 ounces) sour cream
1 cup (4 ounces) shredded cheddar cheese
1 cup (4 ounces) shredded mozzarella cheese
Additional salsa and sour cream, optional

In a skillet, saute onion, green pepper and garlic in oil until tender. Add the corn, chives, cilantro, salt and pepper. Cook until heated through, about 3 minutes. Stir in eggs; cook until completely set, stirring occasionally. Remove from the heat.

Place one tortilla on a lightly greased baking sheet or pizza pan; top with a third of the corn mixture, salsa and sour cream. Sprinkle with a fourth of the cheeses. Repeat layers twice. Top with the remaining tortilla and cheeses. Bake at 350° for 10 minutes or until the cheese is melted. Cut into wedges. Serve with salsa and sour cream if desired. **Yield:** 6-8 servings.

Cheesy Zucchini Saute
Golden Squash Pie
Baked Chicken and Acorn Squash

Chapter 9
Squash & Zucchini

Cheesy Zucchini Saute

(Pictured at left)

Although I no longer have a garden of my own, friends and neighbors keep me amply supplied with squash. As a thank-you, I tell them how to make this refreshing zucchini saute. It's quick, easy and oh, so tasty!
—Doris Biggs, Felton, Delaware

    1/2 cup chopped onion
    1/4 cup butter
      3 cups coarsely shredded zucchini
      2 teaspoons minced fresh basil *or* 1/2
        teaspoon dried basil
    1/2 teaspoon salt
    1/8 teaspoon garlic powder
      1 cup (4 ounces) shredded cheddar
        cheese
      1 cup diced fresh tomato
      2 tablespoons sliced ripe olives

In a large skillet, saute onion in butter until crisp-tender. Stir in zucchini, basil, salt and garlic powder. Cook and stir for 4-5 minutes or until zucchini is crisp-tender. Sprinkle with the cheese, tomato and olives. Cover and cook for 4-5 minutes or until cheese is melted. Serve immediately. **Yield:** 6 servings.

Baked Chicken and Acorn Squash

(Pictured at left)

This eye-pleasing main dish is ideal for harvesttime with its colorful acorn squash and sweet peaches. The fragrance of rosemary-seasoned chicken baking is heavenly. My family says it's every bit as delicious as it smells. *—Connie Svoboda, Elko, Minnesota*

      2 small acorn squash (1-1/4 pounds *each*)
      2 to 4 garlic cloves, minced
      2 tablespoons vegetable oil, *divided*
      4 chicken drumsticks
      4 chicken thighs
    1/4 cup packed brown sugar
      1 teaspoon salt
      1 tablespoon minced fresh rosemary
        or 1 teaspoon dried rosemary, crushed
      1 can (15-1/4 ounces) sliced peaches,
        undrained

Cut squash in half lengthwise; discard seeds. Cut each half widthwise into 1/2-in. slices; discard ends. Place slices in an ungreased 13-in. x 9-in. x 2-in. baking dish. Sprinkle with garlic; drizzle with 1 tablespoon oil. In a skillet, brown chicken in remaining oil. Arrange chicken over squash. Combine brown sugar, salt and rosemary; sprinkle over chicken.

Bake, uncovered, at 350° for 45 minutes, basting with pan juices twice. Pour peaches over chicken and squash. Bake, uncovered, 15 minutes longer or until chicken juices run clear and peaches are heated through. **Yield:** 4 servings.

Zucchini Clues

When preparing my favorite Italian or Mexican recipes, I often substitute shredded zucchini for half of the ground beef or sausage. It reduces the fat.   *—Trudy Overlin Rigby, Idaho*

Zucchini is wonderful stuffed and baked. Cut in half lengthwise, and scoop out the flesh, leaving a 1/2-inch shell. Chop the zucchini flesh and combine with sauteed onions, bell peppers and bread crumbs. Add some chopped tomatoes, season to taste and fill the shells. Bake at 400° for about 30 minutes. *—Gale Narlock, Wausau, Wisconsin*

Pineapple Zucchini Bread

Golden Squash Pie

(Pictured on page 62)

Whether you take this yummy pie to a party or potluck, be prepared to share the recipe. An alternative to pumpkin pie, it bakes up high and flavorful.
—Patricia Hardin, Seymour, Tennessee

    4 eggs
    4 cups mashed cooked butternut squash
    1 cup buttermilk
 1/4 cup butter, melted
    2 teaspoons vanilla extract
    2 cups sugar
    2 tablespoons all-purpose flour
    1 teaspoon salt
 1/2 teaspoon baking soda
    2 unbaked pastry shells (9 inches)
Ground nutmeg, optional

In a bowl, combine the eggs, squash, buttermilk, butter and vanilla. Combine the dry ingredients; add to the squash mixture and mix until smooth. Pour into pastry shells. Cover edges loosely with foil.

Bake at 350° for 35 minutes. Remove foil. Bake 25 minutes longer or until a knife inserted near the center comes out clean. Cool on a wire rack. Sprinkle with nutmeg if desired. Store in the refrigerator. **Yield:** 2 pies (6-8 servings each).

Pineapple Zucchini Bread

(Pictured above)

Meals are even more memorable when I complement them with this light garden-fresh bread. The zucchini makes it so moist and tender...and the pineapple lends a delicate tropical twist to every delicious slice. I often share the second loaf. —Shirley Boulet
Whitefield, New Hampshire

    3 eggs
    2 cups finely shredded zucchini
    1 cup vegetable oil
    1 can (8 ounces) crushed pineapple,
      drained
    2 teaspoons vanilla extract
    3 cups all-purpose flour
    2 cups sugar
    2 teaspoons baking soda
1-1/2 teaspoons ground cinnamon
    1 teaspoon salt
  3/4 teaspoon ground nutmeg
  1/2 teaspoon baking powder
    1 cup chopped nuts
    1 cup raisins *or* currants, optional

In a bowl, combine the eggs, zucchini, oil, pineapple and vanilla. Combine the dry ingredients; stir into egg mixture just until moistened. Fold in nuts and raisins if desired.

Pour into two greased 8-in. x 4-in. x 2-in. loaf pans. Bake at 350° for 50-60 minutes or until a toothpick inserted near the center comes out clean. Cool for 10 minutes before removing from pans to wire racks. **Yield:** 2 loaves.

Lemony Acorn Slices

I have used this recipe often over the years. With the skins on the sliced squash and lemon sauce drizzled over it, this side dish looks as good as it tastes.
—Nell Fletcher, Sedalia, Colorado

    2 large acorn squash (2-1/4 pounds *each*)
    1 cup plus 2 tablespoons water, *divided*
  1/2 cup sugar
    2 tablespoons lemon juice
    1 tablespoon butter
  1/4 teaspoon salt
  1/8 teaspoon pepper
Lemon wedges and fresh mint, optional

Wash squash. Cut in half lengthwise; remove and discard the seeds and membrane. Cut each half crosswise into 1/2-in. slices; discard ends. Place slices in a large skillet. Add 1 cup water; bring to a boil. Reduce heat; cover and simmer for 20 minutes or until tender.

Meanwhile, in a heavy saucepan, combine the sugar and remaining water. Cook over medium heat until sugar melts and syrup is golden, stirring occasionally. Remove from the heat; carefully add lemon juice, butter, salt and pepper. Cook and stir over low heat until butter melts. Place squash on a serving plate; top with syrup. Garnish with lemon and mint if desired. **Yield:** 6 servings.

Zucchini Garden Chowder

When our kids were young, they were reluctant to try new things. But they loved the addition of zucchini to my chowder! —Nanette Jordan, Canton, Michigan

2 medium zucchini, chopped
1 medium onion, chopped
2 tablespoons minced fresh parsley
1 teaspoon dried basil
1/3 cup butter
1/3 cup all-purpose flour
1 teaspoon salt
1/4 teaspoon pepper
3 cups water
3 chicken bouillon cubes
1 teaspoon lemon juice
1 can (14-1/2 ounces) diced tomatoes, undrained
1 can (12 ounces) evaporated milk
1 package (10 ounces) frozen corn
1/4 cup grated Parmesan cheese
2 cups (8 ounces) shredded cheddar cheese
Pinch sugar, optional
Additional chopped parsley, optional

In a Dutch oven or soup kettle over medium heat, saute the zucchini, onion, parsley and basil in butter until vegetables are tender. Stir in flour, salt and pepper. Gradually stir in water. Add the bouillon and lemon juice; mix well.

Bring to a boil; cook and stir for 2 minutes. Add tomatoes, milk and corn; bring to a boil. Reduce heat; cover and simmer for 5 minutes or until corn is tender. Just before serving, stir in cheeses until melted. Add sugar and garnish with parsley if desired. **Yield:** 8-10 servings (about 2-1/2 quarts).

Zesty Gazpacho Salad

This refreshing salad is excellent for a summer cookout. You mix it ahead, so the flavors have time to blend. —Teresa Fischer, Munster, Indiana

2 medium zucchini, chopped
2 medium tomatoes, chopped
1 small ripe avocado, chopped
1 cup fresh *or* frozen corn, thawed
1/2 cup thinly sliced green onions
1/2 cup picante sauce
2 tablespoons minced fresh parsley
2 tablespoons lemon juice
1 tablespoon vegetable oil
3/4 teaspoon garlic salt
1/4 teaspoon ground cumin

In a bowl, combine the first five ingredients. In a small bowl, combine remaining ingredients; mix well. Pour over zucchini mixture; toss to coat. Cover and refrigerate for at least 4 hours. **Yield:** 8-10 servings.

Toasted Zucchini Snacks

(Pictured below)

I added green pepper to this recipe I got years ago from a friend. I prepare this rich snack for company when zucchini is plentiful. Everyone seems to enjoy it— even those who say they don't care for zucchini. —Jane Bone, Cape Coral, Florida

2 cups shredded zucchini
1 teaspoon salt
1/2 cup mayonnaise
1/2 cup plain yogurt
1/4 cup grated Parmesan cheese
1/4 cup finely chopped green pepper
4 green onions, thinly sliced
1 garlic clove, minced
1 teaspoon Worcestershire sauce
1/4 teaspoon hot pepper sauce
36 slices snack rye bread

In a bowl, toss the zucchini and salt; let stand for 1 hour. Rinse and drain, pressing out excess liquid. Add the next eight ingredients; stir until combined. Spread a rounded teaspoonful on each slice of bread; place on a baking sheet. Bake at 375° for 10-12 minutes or until bubbly. Serve hot. **Yield:** 3 dozen.

Toasted Zucchini Snacks

Grilled Dijon Summer Squash

(Pictured above)

A niece gave this mustard-seasoned squash recipe to me. My husband, Doug, and our three grandchildren love the zesty flavor and slightly crunchy texture. The veggies are perfect partners to any grilled meat and re-heat easily. —Ruth Lee, Troy, Ontario

- 1/2 cup olive oil
- 1/4 cup red wine vinegar
- 1 tablespoon minced fresh oregano *or* 1 teaspoon dried oregano
- 1 tablespoon Dijon mustard
- 2 garlic cloves, minced
- 1/2 teaspoon salt
- 1/4 teaspoon pepper
- 4 medium zucchini, cut into 1/2-inch slices
- 4 medium yellow squash, cut into 1/2-inch slices
- 2 medium red onions, quartered
- 1 large sweet red pepper, cut into 2-inch pieces
- 1 large sweet yellow pepper, cut into 2-inch pieces
- 12 to 16 whole fresh mushrooms
- 12 cherry tomatoes

In a jar with a tight-fitting lid, combine the oil, vinegar, oregano, mustard, garlic, salt and pepper. Place the vegetables in a shallow baking dish. Add marinade and toss to coat.

Let stand for 15 minutes. Drain and discard marinade; arrange vegetables on a vegetable grill rack. Grill, covered, over indirect heat for 10-12 minutes or until tender. **Yield:** 16-18 servings.

Zucchini Frittata

Zucchini is delicious...and especially abundant come summer. This mouth-watering dish can be on the break-fast table in a hurry! —Mildred Fox, Fostoria, Ohio

- 4 cups diced zucchini
- 1 small onion, chopped

4 eggs
1 cup (4 ounces) shredded cheddar cheese
1 cup cubed fully cooked ham
3/4 teaspoon salt
1/8 teaspoon pepper

In a 9-in. microwave-safe pie plate, combine the zucchini and onion. Cover and microwave on high for 5 minutes or until tender; drain.

In a bowl, combine the eggs, cheese, ham, salt and pepper. Carefully pour over zucchini mixture. Microwave at 70% power for 11-12 minutes or until a knife inserted near the center comes out clean. **Yield:** 6 servings.

Editor's Note: This recipe was tested in an 850-watt microwave.

Zucchini Cupcakes

These irresistible cupcakes are so good, you actually forget you're eating your vegetables, too.
—Virginia Breitmeyer, Craftsbury, Vermont

3 eggs
1-1/3 cups sugar
1/2 cup vegetable oil
1/2 cup orange juice
1 teaspoon almond extract
2-1/2 cups all-purpose flour
2 teaspoons ground cinnamon
2 teaspoons baking powder
1 teaspoon baking soda
1 teaspoon salt
1/2 teaspoon ground cloves
1-1/2 cups shredded zucchini
CARAMEL FROSTING:
1 cup packed brown sugar
1/2 cup butter
1/4 cup milk
1 teaspoon vanilla extract
1-1/2 to 2 cups confectioners' sugar

In a mixing bowl, beat eggs, sugar, oil, orange juice and extract. Combine dry ingredients; add to the egg mixture. Mix well. Add zucchini; mix well. Fill greased or paper-lined muffin cups two-thirds full. Bake at 350° for 20-25 minutes or until a toothpick inserted near the center comes out clean. Cool for 10 minutes before removing to a wire rack.

In a saucepan, combine brown sugar, butter and milk; bring to a boil over medium heat. Cook and stir for 2 minutes. Remove from heat; stir in vanilla. Cool to lukewarm. Gradually beat in confectioners' sugar until frosting reaches spreading consistency. Frost cupcakes. **Yield:** 1-1/2 to 2 dozen.

Navy Bean Squash Soup

(Pictured below)

On a chilly day, what could be more comforting than a pot of this homemade soup simmering on the stove? The mix of ham, beans and squash is such a hearty combination, you'll savor every steamy spoonful.
—Linda Eggers, Albany, California

1 pound dry navy beans, sorted and rinsed
2 cans (14-1/2 ounces *each*) chicken broth
2 cups water
1 meaty ham bone
2 to 2-1/2 pounds butternut squash, peeled, seeded and cubed
1 large onion, chopped
1/2 teaspoon salt
1/2 teaspoon pepper

Place beans in a large saucepan or Dutch oven; add water to cover by 2 in. Bring to a boil; boil for 2 minutes. Remove from the heat; cover and let stand for 1 hour. Drain and discard liquid; return beans to pan. Add the broth, water, ham bone, squash, onion, salt and pepper. Bring to a boil. Reduce heat; cover and simmer for 1-1/2 to 1-3/4 hours or until beans are tender.

Remove ham bone. Mash the soup mixture, leaving some chunks if desired. Remove ham from bone; cut into chunks. Discard bone and fat. Return meat to the soup; heat through. **Yield:** 12-14 servings (about 3 quarts).

Navy Bean Squash Soup

Buttercup Squash Coffee Cake

(Pictured below)

My father grows a large squash patch, so each fall, I get an ample amount of his harvest. I make this treat to share with my co-workers. They rave about the moist cake, the crunchy streusel and the applesauce between the layers. —Mary Jones, Cumberland, Maine

STREUSEL:
  1/4 cup packed brown sugar
  1/4 cup sugar
  1/4 cup all-purpose flour
  1/4 cup quick-cooking oats
  1/4 cup chopped nuts
1-1/2 teaspoons ground cinnamon
  3 tablespoons cold butter
CAKE:
  1/2 cup butter-flavored shortening
  1 cup sugar
  2 eggs
  1 cup mashed cooked buttercup squash
  1 teaspoon vanilla extract
  2 cups all-purpose flour
  2 teaspoons baking powder
1-1/2 teaspoons ground cinnamon
  1/2 teaspoon baking soda
  1/2 teaspoon salt
  1/4 teaspoon ground ginger
  1/4 teaspoon ground nutmeg
Pinch ground cloves
  1/2 cup unsweetened applesauce
GLAZE:
  1/2 cup confectioners' sugar
  1/4 teaspoon vanilla extract
1-1/2 teaspoons hot water

Buttercup Squash Coffee Cake

Combine the first six ingredients. Cut in butter until crumbly; set aside. In a mixing bowl, cream shortening and sugar. Beat in eggs, one at a time. Beat in squash and vanilla. Combine dry ingredients; gradually add to creamed mixture.

Spoon half into a greased 9-in. springform pan. Spread applesauce over batter. Sprinkle with half of the streusel. Spoon remaining batter evenly over streusel. Top with remaining streusel. Bake at 350° for 50-55 minutes or until a toothpick comes out clean. Cool for 10 minutes; remove sides of pan. Combine glaze ingredients; drizzle over coffee cake. **Yield:** 10-12 servings.

Where's the Squash Lasagna

I devised this recipe to hide zucchini from my grandchildren and any others who think they don't like it. —Norma Brinson, Greenville, North Carolina

  1 pound ground beef
  2 large zucchini (about 1 pound), shredded
3/4 cup chopped onion
  2 garlic cloves, minced
  1 can (14-1/2 ounces) stewed tomatoes
  2 cups water
  1 can (12 ounces) tomato paste
  1 tablespoon minced fresh parsley
1-1/2 teaspoons salt
  1 teaspoon sugar
  1/2 teaspoon dried oregano
  1/2 teaspoon pepper
  9 lasagna noodles, cooked, rinsed and drained

1 carton (15 ounces) ricotta cheese
2 cups (8 ounces) shredded mozzarella cheese
1 cup grated Parmesan cheese

In a skillet, cook beef, zucchini, onion and garlic over medium heat until meat is no longer pink; drain. Place tomatoes in a food processor or blender; cover and process until smooth. Stir into beef mixture. Add water, tomato paste, parsley and seasonings. Bring to a boil. Reduce heat; simmer, uncovered, for 30 minutes, stirring occasionally.

Spread 1 cup meat sauce in a greased 13-in. x 9-in. x 2-in. baking dish. Arrange three noodles over sauce. Spread with a third of the meat sauce; top with half of the ricotta. Sprinkle with a third of the mozzarella and Parmesan. Repeat. Top with remaining noodles, meat sauce and cheeses.

Cover and bake at 350° for 45 minutes. Uncover and bake 15 minutes longer or until bubbly. Let the dish stand for 15 minutes before cutting. **Yield: 12 servings.**

Cheesy Zucchini Bake

Butternut Squash Dinner Rolls

These wholesome rolls are a pleasant addition to any entree. I get so many requests for them at holiday time, I make about 100 dozen in December. —Ula Kessler
Liberty Center, Ohio

2 tablespoons plus 1 teaspoon active dry yeast
3/4 teaspoon plus 1 cup sugar, *divided*
1/2 cup warm water (110° to 115°)
2 cups warm milk (110° to 115°)
1/4 cup butter, softened
2 cups mashed cooked butternut squash
2 teaspoons salt
1/4 cup wheat germ
10 to 11-1/2 cups all-purpose flour
Additional butter, melted

In a large mixing bowl, dissolve yeast and 3/4 teaspoon sugar in warm water; let stand for 5 minutes. Add the milk, butter, squash, salt and remaining sugar; mix until smooth. Add wheat germ and 4 cups flour; beat until smooth. Stir in enough remaining flour to form a soft dough.

Turn onto a floured surface; knead until smooth and elastic, about 6-8 minutes. Place in a greased bowl, turning once to grease top. Cover and let rise in a warm place until doubled, about 1 hour.

Punch dough down and divide into thirds; divide each portion into 20 pieces. Shape into balls. Place on greased baking sheets. Cover and let rise until doubled, about 30 minutes. Bake at 350° for 15-17 minutes or until golden brown. Brush with butter. Remove to wire racks. **Yield: 5 dozen.**

Cheesy Zucchini Bake

(Pictured above)

Ever since a friend shared this classic casserole with me, I actually look forward to our annual bounty of zucchini. —Sue Stanton, Linville, North Carolina

4-1/2 cups sliced zucchini
2 to 3 tablespoons olive oil
Salt and pepper to taste
1 large onion, chopped
2 tablespoons minced garlic
1 can (10-3/4 ounces) tomato puree
1 can (6 ounces) tomato paste
3 tablespoons sugar
1 teaspoon Italian seasoning
1 teaspoon dried basil
2 cans (2-1/4 ounces each) sliced ripe olives, drained
3 cups (12 ounces) shredded mozzarella cheese
6 eggs, lightly beaten
1-1/2 cups grated Parmesan cheese

In a large skillet, saute zucchini in oil until tender. Sprinkle with salt and pepper; stir. Transfer to an ungreased 13-in. x 9-in. x 2-in. baking dish.

In the same skillet, saute onion until crisp-tender. Add garlic; saute 3 minutes longer. Stir in tomato puree, tomato paste, sugar, Italian seasoning and basil. Bring to a boil. Reduce heat; simmer, uncovered, for 10-15 minutes or until slightly thickened. Stir in olives. Pour over zucchini. Sprinkle with mozzarella.

Combine the eggs and Parmesan cheese; pour over zucchini. Bake, uncovered, at 375° for 25-30 minutes or until a knife inserted near the center comes out clean. Let the dish stand for 15 minutes before serving. **Yield: 12-16 servings.**

Surprise Carrot Cake
Scalloped Carrots
Creamy Carrot Parsnip Soup

Chapter 10
Carrots

Creamy Carrot Parsnip Soup

(Pictured at left)

Our farm family would eat soup every day as long as it didn't come from a can! This smooth creamy concoction tastes like it's fresh from the garden. A subtle hint of horseradish and ginger sparks the tastebuds every steaming spoonful. —Phyllis Clinehens
Maplewood, Ohio

> 8 cups chopped carrots
> 6 cups chopped peeled parsnips
> 4 cups chicken broth
> 3 cups water
> 2 teaspoons sugar
> 1 teaspoon salt
> 1 medium onion, chopped
> 4 garlic cloves, minced
> 1 teaspoon grated fresh horseradish
> 1 teaspoon grated fresh gingerroot
> 3 tablespoons butter
> 2 cups buttermilk
> 2 tablespoons sour cream

Fresh dill sprigs, optional

In a Dutch oven or soup kettle, combine the carrots, parsnips, broth, water, sugar and salt; bring to a boil. Reduce heat; cover and cook for 25-30 minutes or until vegetables are tender.

In a skillet, saute onion, garlic, horseradish and ginger in butter until tender. Add to the carrot mixture. Transfer soup to a blender in batches; cover and process until smooth. Return to the pan. Stir in buttermilk; heat through (do not boil). Garnish servings with sour cream and dill if desired. **Yield:** 12 servings (3 quarts).

Scalloped Carrots

(Pictured at left)

A cookbook my husband gave me as a wedding gift included this recipe—he remembers having the dish as a child at church dinners. Now I make it whenever I need a special vegetable side. It's rich and cheesy even after reheating. —Joyce Tornholm
New Market, Iowa

> 6 cups water
> 12 medium carrots, sliced 1/4 inch thick (about 4 cups)
> 1 medium onion, finely chopped
> 1/2 cup butter, *divided*
> 1/4 cup all-purpose flour
> 1 teaspoon salt
> 1/4 teaspoon ground mustard
> 1/4 teaspoon celery salt

Dash pepper

> 2 cups milk
> 2 cups (8 ounces) shredded cheddar cheese
> 3 slices whole wheat bread, cut into small cubes

In a saucepan, bring water to a boil; add carrots. Return to a boil; cover and cook for 4 minutes. Drain and immediately place the carrots in ice water; drain and pat dry.

In a saucepan, saute onion in 1/4 cup butter. Stir in the flour, salt, mustard, celery salt and pepper until blended. Gradually add milk. Bring to a boil; cook and stir for 2 minutes or until thickened.

In a greased 11-in. x 7-in. x 2-in. baking dish, layer half of the carrots, cheese and white sauce. Repeat layers. Melt remaining butter; toss with bread cubes. Sprinkle over the top. Bake, uncovered, at 350° for 35-40 minutes or until hot and bubbly. **Yield:** 4-6 servings.

Carrot Cues

I've found that a sprinkle of nutmeg enhances the flavor of steamed buttered carrots. —Esther Bane, Glidden, Iowa

Before we freeze our carrots, we cook them in a pressure cooker for 2 minutes, then quickly cool them. They are great in soups and other cooked dishes. —Callie Dalton
Brookfield, Connecticut

Confetti Carrot Fritters

(Pictured below)

Crispy, sweet and savory, these delicate fritters are a fun twist on the traditional fruit-filled variety. They're yummy served with a mustard dipping sauce or drizzle of warm maple syrup, too. —Peggy Camp
Twain, California

      6 cups water
2-1/2 cups finely chopped carrots
    1/4 cup all-purpose flour
    1/4 teaspoon salt
    1/4 teaspoon pepper
      2 eggs, *separated*
      3 tablespoons milk
      2 tablespoons finely chopped onion
      2 tablespoons minced fresh parsley
Vegetable oil for deep-fat frying
MUSTARD SAUCE:
      1 tablespoon minced fresh parsley
      1 tablespoon red wine vinegar
      1 tablespoon Dijon mustard
      1 teaspoon finely chopped green onion
    1/4 cup olive oil

In a saucepan, bring water to a boil; add carrots. Return to a boil; cover and cook for 2 minutes. Drain and immediately place the carrots in ice water; drain and pat dry.

In a bowl, combine the flour, salt and pepper. Combine egg yolks and milk; stir into the flour mixture until smooth. Stir in the onion, parsley and carrots. In a mixing bowl, beat egg whites until stiff peaks form; fold into batter. In an electric skillet, heat 1/4 in. of oil to 375°. Drop batter by 1/3 cupfuls into oil. Fry until golden brown, about 2 minutes on each side.

For mustard sauce, combine the parsley, vinegar, mustard and green onion in a bowl. Slowly whisk in oil until blended. Serve with the fritters. **Yield:** 9 servings.

Surprise Carrot Cake

(Pictured on page 70)

This is a wonderful potluck pleaser with its "surprise" cream cheese center. It's a great way to use up the abundance of carrots from my garden. —Lisa Bowen, Little Britain, Ontario

      3 eggs
1-3/4 cups sugar
      3 cups shredded carrots
      1 cup vegetable oil
      2 cups all-purpose flour
      2 teaspoons baking soda
      2 teaspoons ground cinnamon
      1 teaspoon salt
    1/2 cup chopped pecans
FILLING:
      1 package (8 ounces) cream cheese,
         softened
    1/4 cup sugar
      1 egg
FROSTING:
      1 package (8 ounces) cream cheese,
         softened
    1/4 cup butter, softened
      2 teaspoons vanilla extract
      4 cups confectioners' sugar

In a mixing bowl, beat eggs and sugar. Add carrots and oil; beat until blended. Combine the flour, baking soda, cinnamon and salt. Add to carrot mixture; mix well. Stir in pecans. Pour 3 cups batter into a greased and floured 10-in. fluted tube pan. In a mixing bowl, beat cream cheese and sugar. Add egg; mix well. Spoon over batter. Top with remaining batter.

Bake at 350° for 55-60 minutes or until a toothpick inserted near the center comes out clean. Cool for 10 minutes before removing from pan to a wire rack to cool completely.

For frosting, in a small mixing bowl, beat the cream cheese, butter and vanilla until smooth. Gradually add confectioners' sugar. Frost cake. Store in the refrigerator. **Yield:** 12-16 servings.

Confetti Carrot Fritters

Carrot Mushroom Stir-Fry

When carrots are spruced up as a side dish, they're usually mixed with sweet ingredients. But this savory combination with mushrooms is irresistible.
—*Jacqueline Thompson Graves*
Lawrenceville, Georgia

✓ Uses less fat, sugar or salt. Includes Nutritional Analysis and Diabetic Exchanges.

6 to 8 medium carrots (1 pound), thinly sliced
2 tablespoons butter, optional
2 teaspoons olive oil
1 jar (6 ounces) sliced mushrooms, drained
5 green onions with tops, thinly sliced
1 tablespoon lemon juice
1/2 teaspoon salt, optional
1/4 teaspoon pepper

In a skillet over medium heat, stir-fry carrots in butter if desired and oil for 7 minutes. Add mushrooms and onions; cook and stir for 4-6 minutes or until vegetables are tender. Stir in lemon juice, salt if desired and pepper. **Yield:** 7 servings.

Nutritional Analysis: One 1/2-cup serving (prepared without butter or salt) equals 42 calories, 98 mg sodium, 0 cholesterol, 7 g carbohydrate, 1 g protein, 1 g fat. **Diabetic Exchange:** 1-1/2 vegetable.

Carrot Fruitcake

Start a new holiday tradition with this flavorful golden fruitcake. —*Judy Jungwirth, Athol, South Dakota*

1-1/2 cups vegetable oil
2 cups sugar
4 eggs
3 cups all-purpose flour
2 teaspoons baking powder
2 teaspoons baking soda
2 teaspoons ground cinnamon
1 teaspoon salt
3 cups finely shredded carrots
1-1/2 cups coarsely chopped nuts
1 cup *each* raisins, chopped dates and mixed candied fruit

In a mixing bowl, combine oil and sugar. Add eggs, one at a time, beating well after each. Combine flour, baking powder, baking soda, cinnamon and salt; add to egg mixture. Beat until smooth. Stir in remaining ingredients. Pour into two greased and floured 9-in. x 5-in. x 3-in. loaf pans.

Bake at 350° for 1 hour or until a toothpick inserted near the center comes out clean. Cool in pans for 10 minutes; remove to a wire rack to cool completely. **Yield:** 2 loaves.

Chicken Carrot Fried Rice

Chicken Carrot Fried Rice

(Pictured above)

A dear friend shared this colorful stir-fry when my four children were small. It quickly won over those picky eaters! To cut down on prep time, I make the rice ahead and often marinate the chicken beforehand.
—*Peggy Spieckermann, Joplin, Missouri*

3/4 pound boneless skinless chicken breasts, cubed
4 tablespoons soy sauce, *divided*
2 garlic cloves, minced
1-1/2 cups chopped fresh broccoli
3 green onions, sliced
2 tablespoons vegetable oil, *divided*
3 large carrots, shredded
4 cups cold cooked rice
1/4 teaspoon pepper

In a bowl, combine the chicken, 1 tablespoon soy sauce and garlic; set aside. In a large skillet or wok, stir-fry the broccoli and green onions in 1 tablespoon oil for 5 minutes. Add carrots; stir-fry 4 minutes longer or until crisp-tender. Remove and set aside.

In the same skillet, stir-fry the chicken in remaining oil until no longer pink and chicken juices run clear. Add the rice, pepper, vegetables and remaining soy sauce. Stir-fry until heated through. **Yield:** 4-6 servings.

Pickled Carrots

Pickled Carrots

(Pictured above)

The trick to pickled carrots is cooking them just long enough to retain a harvest-fresh "snap". These tangy treats are terrific for perking up a buffet table or relish tray. —Cecilia Grondin, Grand Falls, New Brunswick

1 pound carrots, cut into 3-inch julienne strips
3/4 cup water
2/3 cup white vinegar
3/4 cup sugar
1 cinnamon stick (3 inches), broken
3 whole cloves
1 tablespoon mustard seed

Place 1 in. of water in a saucepan; add carrots. Bring to a boil. Reduce heat; cover and simmer for 3-4 minutes or until crisp-tender. Drain and rinse in cold water. Place in a bowl and set aside.

In a saucepan, combine water, vinegar, sugar, cinnamon, whole cloves and mustard seed. Bring to a boil. Reduce heat; simmer, uncovered, for 10 minutes. Cool; pour over the carrots. Cover and refrigerate for 8 hours or overnight. Discard cloves and cinnamon. Serve carrots with a slotted spoon. **Yield:** 6-8 servings.

Carrots and Pineapple

This simple side dish had been a favorite with family and friends for years. —Cora Christian, Church Hill, Tennessee

2 cups baby carrots
1 can (20 ounces) pineapple chunks

4 teaspoons cornstarch
1/2 teaspoon ground cinnamon
1/2 cup packed brown sugar
1 tablespoon butter

In a saucepan, bring 1 in. of water to a boil; place carrots in a steamer basket over water. Cover and steam for 8-10 minutes or until crisp-tender. Drain pineapple, reserving juice; set pineapple aside.

In a saucepan, combine cornstarch and cinnamon. Add the brown sugar, butter and reserved juice. Bring to a boil; cook and stir for 2 minutes or until thickened. Stir in the carrots and pineapple; heat through. **Yield:** 4 servings.

Apricot-Orange Glazed Carrots

Looking for an easy way to dress up cooked carrots, I hit on this delicious recipe. The fruity glaze complements the natural sweetness of the carrots. —Joan Huggins, Waynesboro, Mississippi

8 medium carrots, sliced
1/2 cup dried apricots, sliced
1/2 cup orange juice
1 tablespoon butter
1-1/2 teaspoons brown sugar
1/2 teaspoon salt
1/4 teaspoon grated orange peel
1/8 teaspoon ground ginger

Place 1 in. of water in a large saucepan; add carrots. Bring to a boil. Reduce heat; cover and simmer for 9-11 minutes or until crisp-tender. Drain and set aside. In the same pan, combine the remaining ingredients; cook and stir until slightly thickened. Return carrots to the pan; stir until glazed and heated through. **Yield:** 6 servings.

Carrots Supreme

This creamy carrot casserole is always a hit. An easy-to-fix but very special side dish, it goes well with almost any meat or poultry. —Lise Thomson, Magrath, Alberta

8 cups sliced carrots
1 small onion, chopped
1 tablespoon butter
1 can (10-3/4 ounces) condensed cream of mushroom soup, undiluted

1 can (4 ounces) mushroom stems and
  pieces, drained
1/2 cup grated Parmesan cheese
1 cup soft bread crumbs

Place carrots in a saucepan and cover with water. Bring to a boil. Reduce heat; cover and cook until tender. Meanwhile, in a small skillet, saute onion in butter until tender. Drain carrots; add onion, soup, mushrooms and Parmesan cheese. Transfer to a greased 2-1/2-qt. baking dish. Sprinkle with bread crumbs. Bake, uncovered, at 350° for 30-35 minutes or until heated through. **Yield:** 8 servings.

Carrots in Almond Sauce

Here's an easy way to add elegance and flavor to a plain vegetable. The combination of carrots and nuts is delightful. —Carol Anderson, Salt Lake City, Utah

1 pound carrots, julienned
1/2 cup thinly sliced green onions
1/4 cup butter
1 teaspoon cornstarch
1/2 cup water
1/2 teaspoon chicken bouillon granules
1/2 teaspoon dill weed
1/8 teaspoon pepper
1/4 cup sliced almonds, toasted

In a saucepan, cook carrots in a small amount of water until crisp-tender; drain. Transfer to a serving bowl and keep warm.

In the same pan, saute onions in butter until tender. Combine cornstarch and water until smooth; stir into onions. Add bouillon, dill and pepper. Bring to a boil over medium heat; cook and stir for 1 minute or until thickened and bubbly. Stir in almonds. Pour over carrots; stir to coat. **Yield:** 6 servings.

Oven-Roasted Carrots

My family really looks forward to carrots when they're prepared this flavorful way.   —Marlene Schott
                                              Devine, Texas

2 pounds baby carrots
4 small onions, quartered
6 garlic cloves, peeled
2 tablespoons olive oil
2 teaspoons white wine vinegar
1 to 2 teaspoons dried thyme
1/2 teaspoon salt
1/8 teaspoon pepper

Place carrots, onions and garlic in two greased 15-in. x 10-in. x 1-in. baking pans. Drizzle with oil and vinegar. Sprinkle with thyme, salt and pepper

and gently toss to coat.

Cover and bake at 450° for 20 minutes; stir. Bake, uncovered, for 10 minutes; stir again. Bake 10 minutes longer or until carrots are crisp-tender. **Yield:** 8 servings.

Chocolate Chip Carrot Bread

(Pictured below)

My family likes sweet breads, and this loaf incorporates many of their favorite ingredients.
—Sharon Setzer, Philomath, Oregon

3 cups all-purpose flour
1 cup sugar
1 cup packed brown sugar
2 to 3 teaspoons ground cinnamon
2 teaspoons baking powder
1 teaspoon baking soda
1 teaspoon salt
1 teaspoon ground ginger
1/4 to 1/2 teaspoon ground cloves
3 eggs
3/4 cup orange juice
3/4 cup vegetable oil
1 teaspoon vanilla extract
2 cups grated carrots
1 cup (6 ounces) semisweet chocolate
  chips

In a large bowl, combine the first nine ingredients. In a small bowl, beat the eggs, orange juice, oil and vanilla. Stir into the dry ingredients just until moistened. Fold in the carrots and chocolate chips.

Transfer to two greased 8-in. x 4-in. x 2-in. loaf pans. Bake at 350° for 55-60 minutes or until a toothpick comes out clean. Cool for 10 minutes; remove from pans to wire racks. **Yield:** 2 loaves.

Chocolate Chip Carrot Bread

Pork Roast with Apple Topping
Apple Snack Squares
Apple Luncheon Salad
Apple Ladder Loaf

Chapter 11
Apples

Apple Luncheon Salad

(Pictured at left)

Served with fresh bread, this makes a nice light meal. I've also used this recipe for entertaining, and it has always been a success at potluck dinners. It's a delicious way to use up leftover beef. —Audrey Marsh
Arva, Ontario

- 3 cups diced red apples
- 1 cup julienned cooked roast beef
- 1 cup thinly sliced celery
- 4 green onions, thinly sliced
- 1/4 cup minced fresh parsley
- 1/3 cup vegetable oil
- 2 tablespoons cider vinegar
- 1 garlic clove, minced
- 1/2 teaspoon salt
- 1/4 teaspoon pepper
- Lettuce leaves

In a bowl, combine the first five ingredients. In a small bowl, combine oil, vinegar, garlic, salt and pepper; mix well. Pour over apple mixture; toss to coat. Cover and refrigerate for at least 1 hour. Serve on lettuce. **Yield:** 4-6 servings.

Apple Snack Squares

(Pictured at left)

As soon as I was old enough to stand on a chair, I started cooking. This recipe came from my sister-in-law. It's a favorite at our large family gatherings.
—Julia Quintrell, Sumerco, West Virginia

- 2 cups sugar
- 2 eggs
- 3/4 cup vegetable oil
- 2-1/2 cups self-rising flour
- 1 teaspoon ground cinnamon
- 3 cups diced peeled tart apples
- 1 cup chopped walnuts
- 3/4 cup butterscotch chips

In a bowl, combine sugar, eggs and oil; mix well. Stir in flour and cinnamon (batter will be thick). Stir in apples and nuts. Spread into a greased 13-in. x 9-in. x 2-in. baking pan. Sprinkle with chips. Bake at 350° for 35-40 minutes or until golden and a toothpick inserted near the center comes out clean. Cool before cutting. **Yield:** 2 dozen.

Editor's Note: As a substitute for each cup of self-rising flour, place 1-1/2 teaspoons of baking powder and 1/2 teaspoon of salt in a measuring cup. Add all-purpose flour to equal 1 cup.

Pork Roast with Apple Topping

(Pictured at left)

This recipe's one my mother-in-law and I developed together. The topping also goes great with pork chops, ham and lean sausage balls or patties. —Paula Neal
Dolores, Colorado

- 1 boneless pork loin roast (3 to 3-1/2 pounds), trimmed
- 1/2 teaspoon poultry seasoning
- 1 jar (10 ounces) apple jelly
- 1 cup apple juice
- 1/2 teaspoon ground cardamom
- 1 cup chopped peeled tart fresh *or* dried apples
- 3 tablespoons chopped fresh *or* dried cranberries
- 5 teaspoons cornstarch
- 2 tablespoons water

Place roast on a rack in a shallow roasting pan and rub with poultry seasoning. Bake, uncovered, at 325° for 2-1/2 hours or until a meat thermometer reads 160°-170°.

For topping, combine the apple jelly, juice and cardamom in a saucepan. Cook and stir over low heat until smooth. Add apples and cranberries; cook until tender, about 5-10 minutes. Combine cornstarch and water; stir into apple mixture. Bring to a boil. Cook and stir over medium heat until thickened, about 1-2 minutes.

Remove roast from oven and let stand for 10 minutes before slicing. Serve with apple topping. **Yield:** 8-10 servings (about 2 cups topping).

Honey Baked Apples

Honey Baked Apples

(Pictured above)

These tender apples smell so good while they're in the oven—and taste even better. We enjoy the golden raisins inside and the soothing taste of honey. They're a yummy change from the cinnamon and sugar seasoning traditionally used with apples. —Chere Bell Colorado Springs, Colorado

2-1/4 cups water
3/4 cup packed brown sugar
3 tablespoons honey
6 large tart apples
1 cup golden raisins
Vanilla ice cream, optional

In a saucepan, bring water, brown sugar and honey to a boil. Remove from the heat. Core apples and peel the top third of each. Place in an ungreased 9-in. baking dish. Fill apples with raisins; sprinkle any remaining raisins into pan. Pour sugar syrup over apples. Bake, uncovered, at 350° for 1 hour or until tender, basting occasionally. Serve with ice cream if desired. **Yield:** 6 servings.

Apple Ladder Loaf

(Pictured on page 76)

This rich bread with its spicy apple filling makes a nice breakfast pastry or, with a scoop of ice cream, a lovely dessert. —Norma Foster, Compton, Illinois

1 package (1/4 ounce) active dry yeast
1/4 cup warm water (110° to 115°)
1/2 cup warm milk (110° to 115°)
1/2 cup butter, softened
1/3 cup sugar
4 eggs
4-1/2 to 4-3/4 cups all-purpose flour
FILLING:
1/3 cup packed brown sugar
2 tablespoons all-purpose flour
1-1/4 teaspoons ground cinnamon
1/2 teaspoon ground nutmeg
1/8 teaspoon ground allspice
4 cups thinly sliced peeled tart apples
1/4 cup butter, softened
ICING:
1 cup confectioners' sugar
1 to 2 tablespoons orange juice
1/4 teaspoon vanilla extract

In a mixing bowl, dissolve the yeast in water; let stand for 5 minutes. Add the milk, butter, sugar, eggs and 1 cup flour. Beat on low speed for 3 minutes. Stir in enough remaining flour to form a soft dough. Knead on a floured surface until smooth and elastic, about 6-8 minutes. Place dough in a greased bowl, turning once to grease top. Cover and refrigerate for 6-24 hours; punch dough down after 1-2 hours.

For filling, combine sugar, flour, cinnamon, nutmeg and allspice in a small bowl. Add apples; toss to coat. Set aside.

Punch dough down; divide in half. Roll each half into a 12-in. x 9-in. rectangle. Place each rectangle on a greased baking sheet. Spread with butter. Spread filling down center third of each rectangle. On each long side, cut 1-in.-wide strips 3 in. into center. Starting at one end, fold alternating strips at an angle across filling; seal ends. Cover and let rise for 45-60 minutes or until nearly doubled.

Bake at 350° for 25-30 minutes or until golden brown. Combine icing ingredients until smooth; drizzle over warm loaves. Serve warm or at room temperature. **Yield:** 2 loaves.

Tasty Apple Tart

Almost like a pizza, this tart's easy to pick up and eat out of your hand. Kids love it. Like most of my best recipes, it came from my mom. Since it's so pretty, I fix it for fancy gatherings such as ladies get-togethers...but I make it to serve at informal barbecues as well. —Leslie DuPerron, Edmonton, Alberta

1-1/2 cups all-purpose flour
 1/4 teaspoon salt
 1/2 cup cold butter
   6 to 7 tablespoons cold water
   4 tablespoons sugar, *divided*
   6 medium apples, peeled and sliced
   3 tablespoons butter, melted
 1/4 cup apricot jam
   1 tablespoon water

In a bowl, combine flour and salt; cut in cold butter until crumbly. Sprinkle with cold water, 1 tablespoon at a time, and toss with a fork until dough can be formed into a ball. On a floured surface, roll dough into a 13-in. circle. Place on an ungreased 12-in. pizza pan; turn edges under. Sprinkle crust with 2 tablespoons sugar.

Beginning at the outside, arrange apples in a circular pattern, overlapping each slice. Make a second circle facing the opposite direction. Continue alternating directions until crust is covered. Brush apples with melted butter; sprinkle with remaining sugar. Bake at 400° for 40-50 minutes or until apples are tender and crust is golden. Combine jam and water; brush over apples. Serve warm. **Yield:** 12-16 servings.

Apple Cabbage Slaw

Chopped apple adds fruity sweetness, color and crunch to the tangy cabbage in this flavorful slaw. It's a refreshing side dish any time of the year. Mom stored apples and cabbage in the root cellar, so she fixed this dish frequently to feed our big family.
—*Lucile Proctor, Panguitch, Utah*

✓ Uses less fat, sugar or salt. Includes Nutritional Analysis and Diabetic Exchanges.

   6 cups shredded cabbage
   3 medium red apples, chopped
   1 can (5 ounces) evaporated milk
 1/4 cup lemon juice
   2 tablespoons sugar
   2 teaspoons grated onion
   1 teaspoon celery seed
 1/2 teaspoon salt, optional
Dash pepper

In a large bowl, toss the cabbage and apples. In a small bowl, combine the remaining ingredients. Pour over cabbage mixture and toss to coat. Refrigerate until serving. **Yield:** 10 servings.
Nutritional Analysis: One 3/4-cup serving (prepared with fat-free evaporated milk and sugar substitute equivalent to 2 tablespoons sugar and without salt) equals 53 calories, 26 mg sodium, 1 mg cholesterol, 12 g carbohydrate, 2 g protein, trace fat. **Diabetic Exchanges:** 1 vegetable, 1/2 fruit.

Apple Salsa with Cinnamon Chips

(Pictured below)

I've served this treat as an appetizer and a snack. Plus, it's sweet enough to be a dessert. It's easy to transport besides. —*Carolyn Brinkmeyer, Aurora, Colorado*

SALSA:
   2 medium tart apples, chopped
   1 cup chopped strawberries
   2 medium kiwifruit, peeled and chopped
   1 small orange
   2 tablespoons brown sugar
   2 tablespoons apple jelly, melted
CHIPS:
   8 flour tortillas (7 *or* 8 inches)
   1 tablespoon water
 1/4 cup sugar
   2 teaspoons ground cinnamon

In a bowl, combine apples, strawberries and kiwi. Grate orange peel to measure 1-1/2 teaspoons; squeeze juice from orange. Add peel and juice to apple mixture. Stir in brown sugar and jelly.

For the chips, brush tortillas lightly with water. Combine sugar and cinnamon; sprinkle over tortillas. Cut each tortilla into 8 wedges. Place in a single layer on ungreased baking sheets. Bake at 400° for 6-8 minutes or until lightly browned. Cool. Serve with salsa. **Yield:** 4 cups salsa.

Apple Salsa with Cinnamon Chips

Dutch Apple Cake

(Pictured below)

My husband and I came to Canada over 50 years ago from Holland. This recipe, a family favorite, is one I found in a Dutch cookbook. It frequently goes along with me to potluck suppers. —Elizabeth Peters
Martintown, Ontario

 3 medium peeled tart apples, sliced 1/4
   inch thick (3 cups)
 3 tablespoons plus 1 cup sugar, *divided*
 1 teaspoon ground cinnamon
 2/3 cup butter, softened
 4 eggs
 1 teaspoon vanilla extract
 2 cups all-purpose flour
 1/8 teaspoon salt

In a bowl, combine the apples, 3 tablespoons sugar and cinnamon; let stand for 1 hour. In a mixing bowl, cream butter and remaining sugar. Add eggs, one at a time, beating well after each. Add vanilla. Combine flour and salt; gradually add to creamed mixture and beat until smooth.

Pour into a greased 9-in. x 5-in. x 3-in. loaf pan. Push apple slices vertically into batter, placing them close together. Bake at 300° for 1 hour and 40 minutes or until a toothpick inserted near the center comes out clean. Cool for 10 minutes on a wire rack. Remove from pan. Serve warm. **Yield:** 10-12 servings.

Dutch Apple Cake

Apple-of-Your-Eye Cheesecake

My most-often-requested dessert, this exquisite cheesecake with apples, caramel and pecans wins me more compliments than anything else I make. My husband's co-workers love it! —Debbie Wilson
Sellersburg, Indiana

 1 cup graham cracker crumbs
 3 tablespoons sugar
 1/2 teaspoon ground cinnamon
 1/4 cup butter, melted
 2 tablespoons finely chopped pecans
FILLING:
 3 packages (8 ounces *each*) cream
   cheese, softened
 3/4 cup sugar
 3 eggs
 3/4 teaspoon vanilla extract
TOPPING:
 2-1/2 cups chopped peeled apples
 1 tablespoon lemon juice
 1/4 cup sugar
 1/2 teaspoon ground cinnamon
 6 tablespoons caramel ice cream topping,
   divided
Sweetened whipped cream
 2 tablespoons chopped pecans

Combine the first five ingredients; press onto the bottom of a lightly greased 9-in. springform pan. Bake at 350° for 10 minutes; cool.

In a mixing bowl, beat cream cheese and sugar until smooth. Add eggs; beat on low just until combined. Stir in vanilla. Pour over crust. Toss apples with lemon juice, sugar and cinnamon; spoon over filling. Bake at 350° for 55-60 minutes or until center is almost set. Cool on a wire rack for 10 minutes.

Carefully run a knife around edge of pan to loosen. Drizzle with 4 tablespoons caramel topping. Cool for 1 hour. Chill overnight. Remove sides of pan. Just before serving, garnish with whipped cream. Drizzle with remaining caramel; sprinkle with pecans. Store in refrigerator. **Yield:** 12 servings.

Saucy Spiced Apple Pie

My mom's sweet and saucy apple pie earns a lip-smacking salute from everyone who tastes it. Since it's hard to wait for it to cool, I like to serve slices warm with a scoop of French vanilla ice cream on top. —Lisa Jedrzejczak, Capac, Michigan

Pastry for double-crust pie (9 inches)
 1/4 cup butter, softened
 2 cups sugar
 1 egg
 1 egg, *separated*
 1/3 cup unsweetened pineapple juice
 1-1/2 teaspoons vanilla extract

1/3 cup all-purpose flour
1/2 teaspoon ground cinnamon
1/4 teaspoon ground ginger
1/4 teaspoon ground nutmeg
6 cups sliced peeled tart apples
Additional sugar

Line a 9-in. pie plate with bottom pastry; trim even with edge. In a mixing bowl, cream butter and sugar. Add the egg, egg yolk, pineapple juice and vanilla; mix well (mixture will appear curdled). Combine the flour, cinnamon, ginger and nutmeg; add to creamed mixture. Fill crust with apple slices. Top with the creamed mixture.

Roll out remaining pastry to fit top of pie; place over filling. Trim, seal and flute edges. Cut slits in top. Beat egg white; brush over pastry. Sprinkle with additional sugar. Bake at 350° for 55-60 minutes or until crust is golden brown and filling is bubbly. Cool on a wire rack. Refrigerate leftovers. **Yield:** 6-8 servings.

Apple Dumpling Dessert

Apple-Ham Grilled Cheese

After finding this recipe years ago, I altered it to fit our tastes by adding the apples. Our whole family loves them! We look forward to fall when we go out to the orchards to gather the fresh-picked ingredients for pies, cobblers, salads...and, of course, this sandwich.
—Shirley Brazel, Rocklin, California

1 cup chopped tart apples
1/3 cup mayonnaise
1/4 cup finely chopped walnuts
8 slices process American cheese
8 slices sourdough bread
4 slices fully cooked ham
1/4 cup butter, softened

Combine apples, mayonnaise and walnuts. Place a slice of cheese on four slices of bread. Layer each with 1/3 cup of the apple mixture, a slice of ham and another slice of cheese; cover with remaining bread. Butter the outsides of the sandwiches. Cook in a large skillet over medium heat on each side until bread is golden brown and cheese is melted. **Yield:** 4 servings.

Apple Dumpling Dessert

(Pictured above right)

My husband loves apple dumplings, but they take so long. So my daughter created a quick-to-fix variation with a nice bonus: no bites of dry crust without filling since it's all mixed throughout! —Janet Weaver
Wooster, Ohio

PASTRY:
4 cups all-purpose flour
2 teaspoons salt
1-1/3 cups shortening
8 to 9 tablespoons cold water
FILLING:
8 cups chopped peeled tart apples
1/4 cup sugar
3/4 teaspoon ground cinnamon
SYRUP:
2 cups water
1 cup packed brown sugar
Whipped topping *or* vanilla ice cream, optional
Mint leaves, optional

In a bowl, combine flour and salt; cut in shortening until the mixture resembles coarse crumbs. Sprinkle with water, 1 tablespoon at a time, and toss with a fork until dough can be formed into a ball.

Divide dough into four parts. On a lightly floured surface, roll one part to fit the bottom of an ungreased 13-in. x 9-in. x 2-in. baking dish. Place in dish; top with a third of the apples. Combine sugar and cinnamon; sprinkle a third over apples. Repeat layers of pastry, apples and cinnamon-sugar twice. Roll out remaining dough to fit top of dish and place on top. Using a sharp knife, cut 2-in. slits through all layers at once.

For syrup, bring water and sugar to a boil. Cook and stir until sugar is dissolved. Pour over top crust. Bake at 400° for 35-40 minutes or until browned and bubbly. Serve warm with whipped topping or ice cream if desired. Garnish with mint if desired. **Yield:** 12 servings.

Swiss Potato Squares
Baked German Potato Salad
Grilled Three-Cheese Potatoes
Mashed Potato Cinnamon Rolls

Chapter 12
Potatoes & Sweet Potatoes

Swiss Potato Squares

(Pictured at left)

To vary these squares, you can substitute cheddar cheese for the Swiss or try Canadian bacon in place of the ham. However you make them, they taste wonderful reheated in the mircrowave. —Nancy Foust
Stoneboro, Pennsylvania

**8 medium russet potatoes (about 3
   pounds), peeled and cubed**
1/3 cup butter, melted
1 tablespoon minced fresh parsley
1-1/2 teaspoons salt
1/4 teaspoon pepper
1-1/2 cups cubed Swiss cheese
1 cup cubed fully cooked ham
1 small onion, grated
1 teaspoon garlic powder
3 eggs
1/2 cup milk
Paprika

Place potatoes in a saucepan and cover with water. Cover and bring to a boil; cook for 20-25 minutes or until very tender. Drain well. Mash with butter, parsley, salt and pepper.

Spread about 4 cups of the potato mixture onto the bottom and up the sides of a greased 8-in. square baking dish. Combine cheese, ham, onion and garlic powder; spoon into potato shell. Combine eggs and milk; pour over all. Top with remaining potato mixture. Sprinkle with paprika.

Bake, uncovered, at 400° for 45-50 minutes or until golden brown. Let stand 5 minutes before cutting. **Yield:** 8-9 servings.

Baked German Potato Salad

(Pictured at left)

What makes this German potato salad so different is that it's sweet instead of tangy. During the holidays, my family has an annual ham dinner, and I always prepare it. The tastes blend very well. —Julie Myers
Lexington, Ohio

12 medium red potatoes (about 3 pounds)
8 bacon strips
2 medium onions, chopped
3/4 cup packed brown sugar
1/3 cup vinegar
1/3 cup sweet pickle juice
2/3 cup water, *divided*
2 teaspoons dried parsley flakes
1 teaspoon salt
1/2 to 3/4 teaspoon celery seed
4-1/2 teaspoons all-purpose flour

In a saucepan, cook potatoes until just tender; drain. Peel and slice into an ungreased 2-qt. baking dish; set aside. In a skillet, cook bacon until crisp; drain, reserving 2 tablespoons drippings. Crumble bacon and set aside. Saute onions in drippings until tender. Stir in brown sugar, vinegar, pickle juice, 1/2 cup water, parsley, salt and celery seed. Simmer, uncovered, for 5-10 minutes.

Meanwhile, combine flour and remaining water until smooth; stir into onion mixture. Bring to a boil. Cook and stir for 2 minutes or until thickened. Pour over potatoes. Add bacon; gently stir to coat. Bake, uncovered, at 350° for 30 minutes or until heated through. **Yield:** 8-10 servings.

Potato Pointers

Leftover baked potatoes can make good potato salad or soup. —Elsie Keith
Trion, Georgia

To prevent potatoes from darkening when boiling, add a small amount of milk to the water. —Nancy Stratford, Island Park, Idaho

Parmesan Potato Soup

Parmesan Potato Soup

(Pictured above)

Even my husband, who's not much of a soup eater, likes this. Our two boys do, too. With homemade bread and a salad, it's a satisfying meal. —Tami Walters
Kingsport, Tennessee

    4 medium baking potatoes (about 2 pounds)
3/4 cup chopped onion
1/2 cup butter
1/2 cup all-purpose flour
1/2 teaspoon dried basil
1/2 teaspoon seasoned salt
1/4 teaspoon celery salt
1/4 teaspoon garlic powder
1/4 teaspoon onion salt
1/4 teaspoon pepper
1/4 teaspoon rubbed sage
1/4 teaspoon dried thyme
4-1/2 cups chicken broth
    6 cups milk
3/4 to 1 cup grated Parmesan cheese
10 bacon strips, cooked and crumbled

Pierce potatoes with a fork; bake in the oven or microwave until tender. Cool, peel and cube; set aside. In a large Dutch oven or soup kettle over medium heat, saute onion in butter until tender. Stir in flour and seasonings. Gradually add broth, stirring constantly.

    Bring to a boil; cook and stir for 2 minutes. Add potatoes; return to a boil. Reduce heat; cover and simmer for 10 minutes. Add milk and cheese; heat through. Stir in bacon. **Yield:** 10-12 servings.

Grilled Three-Cheese Potatoes

(Pictured on page 82)

While this is delicious grilled, I've also cooked it in the oven at 350° for an hour. Add cubed ham to it and you can serve it as a full-meal main dish.
    —Margaret Hanson-Maddox, Montpelier, Indiana

    6 large potatoes, sliced 1/4 inch thick
2 medium onions, chopped
1/3 cup grated Parmesan cheese
    1 cup (4 ounces) shredded sharp cheddar cheese, *divided*
    1 cup (4 ounces) shredded mozzarella cheese, *divided*
    1 pound sliced bacon, cooked and crumbled
1/4 cup butter, cubed
    1 tablespoon minced fresh *or* **dried chives**
    1 to 2 teaspoons seasoned salt
1/2 teaspoon pepper

Divide the potatoes and onions equally between two pieces of heavy-duty foil (about 18-in. square) that have been coated with nonstick cooking spray. Combine Parmesan cheese and 3/4 cup each cheddar and mozzarella; sprinkle over potatoes and onions. Top with bacon, butter, chives, seasoned salt and pepper.

    Bring opposite ends of foil together over filling; fold down several times. Fold unsealed ends toward filling and crimp tightly. Grill, covered, over medium heat for 35-40 minutes or until potatoes are tender. Remove from the grill. Open foil carefully and sprinkle with remaining cheeses. **Yield:** 6-8 servings.

Mashed Potato Cinnamon Rolls

(Pictured on page 82)

A neighbor gave me the recipe for these yummy rolls. They're warm and wonderful to serve for breakfast or as a treat any time of day. —Christine Duncan
Ellensburg, Washington

    1/2 pound russet potatoes, peeled and quartered
    2 packages (1/4 ounce *each***) active dry yeast**
    2 tablespoons sugar
    2 cups warm water (110° to 115°)
3/4 cup butter, melted
    2 eggs, beaten
3/4 cup sugar
2/3 cup instant nonfat dry milk powder
    1 tablespoon salt

2 teaspoons vanilla extract
8 cups all-purpose flour
FILLING:
1/2 cup butter, melted
3/4 cup packed brown sugar
3 tablespoons ground cinnamon
ICING:
2 cups confectioners' sugar
1/4 cup milk
2 tablespoons butter, melted
1/2 teaspoon vanilla extract

Place potatoes in a saucepan and cover with water. Bring to a boil; cook until tender. Drain, reserving 1/2 cup cooking liquid; set aside. Mash potatoes; set aside 1 cup. (Save remaining potatoes for another use.)

Heat reserved potato liquid to 110°-115°. In a mixing bowl, dissolve yeast and sugar in potato liquid; let stand 10 minutes. Add warm water, mashed potatoes, butter, eggs, sugar, milk powder, salt, vanilla and 5 cups flour; beat until smooth. Add enough remaining flour to form a soft dough.

Turn onto a floured surface; knead until smooth and elastic, 6-8 minutes. Place in a greased bowl; turn once to grease top. Cover and chill overnight. Punch dough down; divide into thirds. On a floured surface, roll each portion into a 12-in. x 8-in. rectangle; spread with butter. Combine brown sugar and cinnamon; sprinkle over the dough. Roll up from a long side; pinch seam to seal.

Cut each into 12 slices; place cut side down in three greased 13-in. x 9-in. x 2-in. baking pans. Cover and let rise until almost doubled, 45 minutes.

Bake at 350° for 25-30 minutes. Combine icing ingredients; drizzle over rolls. **Yield:** 3 dozen.

Cranberry Sweet Potato Muffins

(Pictured below)

Sweet potatoes, cranberries and cinnamon give seasonal appeal to these muffins. —Diane Musil
Lyons, Illinois

1-1/2 cups all-purpose flour
1/2 cup sugar
2 teaspoons baking powder
3/4 teaspoon salt
1/2 teaspoon ground cinnamon
1/2 teaspoon ground nutmeg
1 egg
1/2 cup milk
1/2 cup cold mashed sweet potatoes (without added butter or milk)
1/4 cup butter, melted
1 cup chopped fresh or frozen cranberries

In a bowl, combine flour, sugar, baking powder, salt, cinnamon and nutmeg. In a small bowl, combine egg, milk, sweet potatoes and butter; stir into dry ingredients just until moistened. Stir in cranberries. Fill greased or paper-lined muffin cups half full. Bake at 375° for 18-22 minutes or until a toothpick inserted near center comes out clean. Cool in pan 10 minutes; remove to a wire rack. **Yield:** 1 dozen.

Cranberry Sweet
Potato Muffins

Bacon Potato Pancakes

(Pictured below)

Potatoes are something I can eat any time of day and almost any way. This recipe's one I came up with to go along with pigs in blankets several years ago.
—Linda Hall, Hazel Green, Wisconsin

5 to 6 medium uncooked red potatoes, peeled and shredded (3 cups)
5 bacon strips, cooked and crumbled
1/2 cup chopped onion
2 eggs, beaten
2 tablespoons all-purpose flour
Salt and pepper to taste
Dash ground nutmeg
Oil for frying

Rinse and thoroughly drain potatoes. In a bowl, combine the potatoes, bacon, onion, eggs, flour, salt, pepper and nutmeg. In an electric skillet, heat 1/8 in. of oil to 375°. Drop batter by 2 heaping tablespoonfuls into hot oil. Flatten to form patties. Fry until golden brown; turn and cook the other side. Drain on paper towels. **Yield:** 2 dozen.

Pleasing Potato Pizza

I first heard of this delicious and distinctive pizza when a friend tried it at a restaurant. It sounded great so I experimented to come up with my own recipe. The way the slices disappear, there's no doubt about their popularity. Guests are always excited when my potato pizza is on the menu.
—Barbara Zimmer
Wanless, Manitoba

Bacon Potato Pancakes

3 large potatoes, peeled and cubed
1 tube (10 ounces) refrigerated pizza crust
1/4 cup milk
1/2 teaspoon salt
1 pound sliced bacon, diced
1 large onion, chopped
1/2 cup chopped sweet red pepper
1-1/2 cups (6 ounces) shredded cheddar cheese
1-1/2 cups (6 ounces) shredded mozzarella cheese
Sour cream, optional

Place potatoes in a saucepan and cover with water. Bring to a boil; cook for 20-25 minutes or until very tender. Meanwhile, unroll the pizza crust onto an ungreased 14-in. pizza pan; flatten dough and build up edges slightly. Prick dough several times with a fork. Bake at 350° for 15 minutes or until lightly browned. Cool on a wire rack.

Drain potatoes and transfer to a mixing bowl. Mash with milk and salt until smooth. Spread over crust. In a skillet, partially cook the bacon. Add onion and red pepper; cook until bacon is crisp and vegetables are tender. Drain well; sprinkle over potatoes. Top with cheeses. Bake at 375° for 20 minutes or until cheese is melted. Serve with sour cream if desired. **Yield:** 8 slices.

Fried Sweet Potato Pies

With my dad being a farmer who grew them, sweet potatoes have graced our table for as long as I can recall. The pies, though, resulted from an experiment at a church bake sale when we had excess pastry.
—Marilyn Moseley, Toccoa, Georgia

4-1/2 cups self-rising flour
3 tablespoons sugar
1/2 cup shortening
2 eggs
1 cup milk
FILLING:
3 cups mashed sweet potatoes
2 cups sugar
3 eggs, lightly beaten
1 can (5 ounces) evaporated milk
1/4 cup butter, melted
3 tablespoons all-purpose flour
1 teaspoon vanilla extract
Oil for frying
Confectioners' sugar, optional

In a bowl, combine flour and sugar; cut in shortening until mixture resembles coarse crumbs. Combine eggs and milk; add to crumb mixture, tossing with a fork until a ball forms. Cover and chill several hours.

In a large bowl, combine the seven filling ingredients; stir until smooth. Divide the dough into 25 portions. On a floured surface, roll each portion into a 5-in. circle. Spoon 2 tablespoons of filling on half of each circle. Moisten edges with water; fold dough over filling and press edges with a fork to seal. Prick tops with a fork 4-5 times.

In an electric skillet, heat 1/2 in. of oil to 375°. Fry pies, a few at a time, for 1 minute on each side or until golden brown. Drain on paper towels. Dust with confectioners' sugar if desired. Store in the refrigerator. **Yield:** 25 pies.

Editor's Note: As a substitute for each cup of self-rising flour, place 1-1/2 teaspoons baking powder and 1/2 teaspoon salt in a measuring cup. Add all-purpose flour to equal 1 cup. For 1/2 cup of self-rising flour, place 3/4 teaspoon baking powder and 1/4 teaspoon salt in a measuring cup; add all-purpose flour to equal 1/2 cup.

Sweet Potato Dessert Squares

I prepare sweet potatoes every week for my family, mostly as a side dish. But I've found this vegetable also makes desserts even more delightful.
—*Betty Janway, Ruston, Louisiana*

    1 package (18-1/4 ounces) yellow cake
       mix, *divided*
1/2 cup butter, melted
    1 egg, beaten
FILLING:
    3 cups cold mashed sweet potatoes
       (without added milk *or* butter)
2/3 cup milk
1/2 cup packed brown sugar
    2 eggs, beaten
    1 tablespoon pumpkin pie spice
TOPPING:
    6 tablespoons butter
    1 cup chopped pecans
1/4 cup sugar
    1 teaspoon ground cinnamon
Whipped cream and pecan halves, optional

Set aside 1 cup of the cake mix. Combine remaining mix with butter and egg; spread into a greased 13-in. x 9-in. x 2-in. baking pan. Whisk filling ingredients until smooth; pour over crust.

For topping, cut butter into reserved cake mix until crumbly. Stir in pecans, sugar and cinnamon; sprinkle over the filling. Bake at 350° for 60-65 minutes or until a knife inserted near the center comes out clean. Cool. Garnish with whipped cream and pecan halves if desired. **Yield:** 16 servings.

Taco Tater Skins

Taco Tater Skins

(Pictured above)

The idea for my recipe started with a demonstration I didn't like. That version used things most people don't have on hand. I decided to experiment, and out came Taco Tater Skins. —*Phyllis Douglas, Fairview, Michigan*

    6 large russet potatoes
1/2 cup butter, melted
    2 tablespoons taco seasoning
    1 cup (4 ounces) shredded cheddar
       cheese
   15 bacon strips, cooked and crumbled
    3 green onions, chopped
Salsa *and/or* sour cream, optional

Bake potatoes at 375° for 1 hour or until tender. Reduce heat to 350°. When cool enough, cut the potatoes lengthwise into quarters. Scoop out pulp, leaving a 1/4-in. shell (save pulp for another use).

Combine the butter and taco seasoning; brush over both sides of potato skins. Place skin side down on a greased baking sheet. Sprinkle with cheese, bacon and onions. Bake for 5-10 minutes or until the cheese is melted. Serve with salsa and/or sour cream if desired. **Yield:** 2 dozen.

What's in a Name?
Yams are a variety of sweet potato with a vivid orange color, a soft moist consistency and a very sweet flavor. Sweet potatoes are lighter skinned with pale yellow flesh and a firmer, drier texture.

Cheesy Potato Bread

Cheesy Potato Bread

(Pictured above)

Two crusty golden-brown loaves with terrific flavor and texture are what you'll get when you try this recipe. Potatoes and cheese make an unusual but delicious combination for a yeast bread. My family loves it served with soup or stew on cold days. —Deb Amrine
Grand Haven, Michigan

    2 packages (1/4 ounce *each*) active dry yeast
    2 tablespoons sugar
  1/2 cup warm water (110° to 115°)
    1 cup half-and-half cream
    5 tablespoons butter, melted, *divided*
    1 tablespoon salt
  1/8 teaspoon cayenne pepper
5-1/2 to 6 cups all-purpose flour
    2 cups finely shredded peeled potatoes
    1 cup (4 ounces) shredded cheddar cheese

In a large mixing bowl, dissolve the yeast and sugar in warm water; let stand until foamy, about 5 minutes. Add cream, 3 tablespoons butter, salt, cayenne pepper and 2-1/2 cups flour; beat on medium for 2 minutes. Stir in potatoes and enough remaining flour to form a soft dough.

Turn onto a floured surface; knead until smooth and elastic, about 8-10 minutes. (Dough will feel slightly sticky.) Place in a greased bowl, turning once to grease top. Cover and let rise in a warm place until almost doubled, about 1 hour.

Punch the dough down. Pat into a 1/2-in.-thick rectangle. Sprinkle cheese evenly over dough. Fold dough over the cheese and knead into dough.

Shape into two round loaves; place in greased 9-in. round baking pans. Cover and let rise until doubled, about 45 minutes. Cut an X on top of each loaf; brush with remaining butter. Bake at 400° for 35-40 minutes or until golden brown. Remove from pans to cool on wire racks. **Yield:** 2 loaves.

Potato Dumplings

These moist dumplings are an extra-special way to serve potatoes. The bread centers add a comforting touch, and the potato taste really comes through.
—Karin Cousineau, Burlington, North Carolina

    5 to 6 medium potatoes
    5 tablespoons all-purpose flour
    1 egg, beaten
1-1/2 teaspoons salt
  1/4 teaspoon ground nutmeg
    2 slices white bread, toasted
  1/3 cup mashed potato flakes, optional
Melted butter and toasted bread crumbs, optional

Cook potatoes in salted water just until tender; drain. Refrigerate for 2 hours or overnight. Peel and grate potatoes. In a bowl, combine the flour, egg, salt and nutmeg. Add potatoes and mix until a stiff batter is formed, adding additional flour if necessary.

Slice toasted bread into 24 squares, 1/2 in. each; shape 2 tablespoons of the potato mixture around two bread squares, forming a 2-in. ball. In a large kettle, bring salted water to a boil; add a test dumpling. Return to a boil; reduce heat. Cover and simmer for 15-20 minutes or until dumpling is no longer sticky in the center.

If test dumpling falls apart during cooking, add the mashed potato flakes to the batter. Let batter sit for 5 minutes; form remaining dumplings. Add to boiling water; return to a boil and follow the same cooking procedure. Remove dumplings with a slotted spoon to a serving bowl. If desired, drizzle with butter and sprinkle with crumbs. **Yield:** 6-8 servings.

Cheddar Potato Strips

This easy dish wins compliments every time I serve it to family and guests. Fresh parsley adds flavor.
—Lucinda Walker, Somerset, Pennsylvania

    3 large potatoes, cut into 1/2-inch strips
  1/2 cup milk
    1 tablespoon butter
Salt and pepper to taste
  1/2 cup shredded cheddar cheese
    1 tablespoon minced fresh parsley

In a greased 13-in. x 9-in. x 2-in. baking dish, arrange potatoes in a single layer. Pour milk over potatoes. Dot with butter; sprinkle with salt and pepper. Cover and bake at 425° for 30 minutes or until the potatoes are tender. Sprinkle with cheese and parsley. Bake, uncovered, 5 minutes longer or until cheese is melted. **Yield:** 4 servings.

Tropical Sweet Potatoes

Sweet potatoes take on a tropical twist with crushed pineapple mixed in. I add a crumb topping, which bakes to a pretty golden color, and a fresh pineapple garnish. —Mary Gaylord, Balsam Lake, Wisconsin

> 4 large sweet potatoes (3-1/2 pounds)
> 1 can (8 ounces) crushed pineapple, undrained
> 6 tablespoons butter, melted, *divided*
> 3/4 teaspoon salt
> Pinch pepper
> 1/2 cup crushed saltines
> 2 tablespoons brown sugar
> Pinch cloves

In a large saucepan, cover sweet potatoes with water; bring to a boil. Reduce heat; cover and simmer for 30 minutes or until tender. Drain and cool. Peel the potatoes and place in a mixing bowl; mash.

Add the pineapple, 2 tablespoons butter, salt and pepper; mix well. Transfer to a greased 2-qt. baking dish. Combine saltines, brown sugar, cloves and remaining butter; sprinkle over potatoes. Bake, uncovered, at 375° for 30 minutes. **Yield:** 8-10 servings.

Potato Tossed Salad

Instead of serving potato salad plus a tossed salad, I combine the two into one unique and colorful recipe that's met with many compliments. The red potatoes take on added flavor as they marinate.
—Priscilla Weaver, Hagerstown, Maryland

> 1/2 cup olive oil
> 2 tablespoons lemon juice
> 2 teaspoons dried oregano
> 1 garlic clove, minced
> 1/4 teaspoon salt
> 1/2 pound small red potatoes, cooked, peeled and sliced
> 6 cups torn mixed salad greens
> 2 small tomatoes, cut into wedges
> 1 small cucumber, thinly sliced
> 1 small red onion, thinly sliced into rings
> 1/2 cup crumbled feta cheese

In a small bowl, whisk together the first five ingredients. Add potatoes and toss gently. Cover and refrigerate 1 hour. Drain, reserving dressing. Place salad greens in a large bowl. Arrange tomatoes, cucumber, onion, cheese and potatoes on top. Drizzle with the reserved dressing. **Yield:** 8 servings.

Two-Tone Baked Potatoes

(Pictured below)

One potato...two potato...this recipe is doubly wonderful as far as spud lovers are concerned. I have a reputation at home and at work for trying out new recipes. Everyone is glad I took a chance on this one.
—Sherree Stahn, Central City, Nebraska

> 6 medium russet potatoes
> 6 medium sweet potatoes
> 2/3 cup sour cream, *divided*
> 1/3 cup milk
> 3/4 cup shredded cheddar cheese
> 4 tablespoons minced chives, *divided*
> 1-1/2 teaspoons salt, *divided*

Pierce russet and sweet potatoes with a fork. Bake at 400° for 60-70 minutes or until tender. Set sweet potatoes aside. Cut a third off the top of each russet potato; scoop out pulp, leaving skins intact. Place pulp in a bowl; mash with 1/3 cup sour cream, milk, cheese, 2 tablespoons chives and 3/4 teaspoon salt. Set aside.

Cut off the top of each sweet potato; scoop out pulp, leaving skins intact. Mash pulp with remaining sour cream, chives and salt. Stuff mixture into half of each potato skin; spoon russet potato filling into other half. Place on a baking sheet. Bake at 350° for 15-20 minutes or until heated through. **Yield:** 12 servings.

Two-Tone Baked Potatoes

Stuffed Whole Cabbage
Spinach Slaw
Country Pork 'n' Sauerkraut
Creamed Cabbage Soup

Chapter 13
Cabbage

Creamed Cabbage Soup

(Pictured at left)

Although we live in town, we have a big garden. I love planting flowers and vegetables and watching them grow. I even enjoy pulling weeds...honestly! This soup is a favorite way to put my cabbage to use.
—Laurie Harms, Grinnell, Iowa

  2 cans (14-1/2 ounces *each*) chicken broth
  2 celery ribs, chopped
  1 medium head cabbage, shredded
  1 medium onion, chopped
  1 carrot, chopped
1/4 cup butter
  3 tablespoons all-purpose flour
  1 teaspoon salt
1/4 teaspoon pepper
  2 cups half-and-half cream
  1 cup milk
  2 cups cubed fully cooked ham
1/2 teaspoon dried thyme
Chopped fresh parsley

In a large soup kettle or Dutch oven, combine broth, celery, cabbage, onion and carrot; bring to a boil. Reduce heat; cover and simmer for 15-20 minutes or until vegetables are tender.

Meanwhile, melt butter in a medium saucepan. Add flour, salt and pepper; stir to form a smooth paste. Combine cream and milk; gradually add to flour mixture, stirring constantly. Cook and stir until thickened; continue cooking 1 minute longer. Gradually stir into vegetable mixture. Add ham and thyme and heat through. Garnish with parsley. **Yield:** 8-10 servings.

Spinach Slaw

(Pictured at left)

Served with rolls or homemade bread, this slaw's hearty enough to be a main course. Of course, it's also a great side dish—my family especially likes it accompanying steak and corn on the cob. It tastes good with ribs besides. Even people who don't enjoy cabbage like it prepared this way. —GaleLynn Peterson
Long Beach, California

  8 cups shredded iceberg lettuce
  5 cups shredded spinach
  4 cups shredded red cabbage
  3 cups shredded green cabbage
  1 cup mayonnaise
1/4 cup honey
3/4 to 1 teaspoon garlic powder
1/2 teaspoon salt
1/4 teaspoon pepper

In a large bowl, toss lettuce, spinach and cabbage; cover and refrigerate. In a small bowl, combine remaining ingredients; cover and refrigerate. Just before serving, pour dressing over the salad and toss to coat. **Yield:** 12-16 servings.

Country Pork 'n' Sauerkraut

(Pictured at left)

The "secret ingredient" in this recipe is the applesauce. When everything's cooked up, you wouldn't know it's in there...yet the taste's just a bit sweeter. I adapted this recipe from one my mom and grandmother used to make. —Donna Hellendrung
Minneapolis, Minnesota

  2 pounds country-style pork ribs
  1 medium onion, chopped
  1 tablespoon vegetable oil
  1 can (14 ounces) sauerkraut, undrained
  1 cup applesauce
  2 tablespoons brown sugar
  2 teaspoons caraway seed
  1 teaspoon garlic powder
1/2 teaspoon pepper

In a Dutch oven, cook ribs and onion in oil until ribs are browned and onion is tender. Remove from the heat. Combine remaining ingredients and pour over ribs. Cover and bake at 350° for 1-1/2 to 2 hours or until ribs are tender. **Yield:** 4 servings.

Stuffed Whole Cabbage

(Pictured on page 90)

My husband's great about trying new recipes—like this one I experimented with before getting it just right!
—Wyn Jespersen, Suffield, Connecticut

SAUCE:
- 1 can (28 ounces) diced tomatoes, undrained
- 1 can (6 ounces) tomato paste
- 1 garlic clove, minced
- 1-1/2 teaspoons dried oregano
- 1 teaspoon dried thyme
- 1 teaspoon brown sugar
- 1/2 teaspoon salt

FILLING:
- 1 pound ground beef
- 1 medium onion, chopped
- 1 large head cabbage (4 pounds)
- 3/4 cup cooked rice
- 1 egg, beaten
- 1 teaspoon salt
- 1/2 teaspoon pepper
- 2-1/4 cups water, *divided*
- 3 tablespoons cornstarch
- 2 tablespoons shredded Parmesan cheese

Combine sauce ingredients; set aside. In a skillet, cook beef and onion over medium heat until meat is no longer pink and onion is tender; drain. Leaving a 1-in. shell and the core intact, cut out and chop the inside of the cabbage. To beef, add 1 cup chopped cabbage, 1 cup sauce, rice, egg, salt and pepper; mix well. Spoon into cabbage shell.

Place 2 cups water, the remaining chopped cabbage and the remaining sauce in a Dutch oven; mix well. Carefully add stuffed cabbage, meat side up. Cover and bring to a boil. Reduce heat; cover and simmer 1-1/2 hours or until whole cabbage is tender. Remove cabbage to a serving platter and keep warm. Combine the cornstarch and remaining water; add to Dutch oven. Bring to a boil, stirring con-

stantly; boil for 2 minutes. Pour over the cabbage; sprinkle with Parmesan cheese. Cut into wedges to serve. **Yield:** 8 servings.

Cheddar Cabbage Wedges

(Pictured below left)

Whether it's a simple meal or an elaborate Sunday dinner that you are fixing, this side dish adds so much to it.
—Karren Fairbanks, Salt Lake City, Utah

- 1 medium head cabbage (3 pounds)
- 1/2 cup chopped green pepper
- 1/4 cup chopped onion
- 1/4 cup butter
- 1/4 cup all-purpose flour
- 1/2 teaspoon salt
- 1/8 teaspoon pepper
- 2 cups milk
- 3/4 cup shredded cheddar cheese
- 1/2 cup mayonnaise
- 3 tablespoons chili sauce

Cut the cabbage into eight wedges, leaving a portion of the core on each wedge. Steam wedges in boiling salted water in a large kettle or Dutch oven for 10-15 minutes or until crisp-tender. Drain; remove core. Place the wedges in a greased 3-qt. baking dish.

In a medium saucepan, saute the green pepper and onion in butter until tender. Stir in flour, salt and pepper and cook until bubbly. Gradually add milk; cook and stir until thickened. Pour over cabbage.

Bake, uncovered, at 375° for 15 minutes. In a small bowl, combine cheese, mayonnaise and chili sauce; spoon over wedges. Return to the oven for 5 minutes. **Yield:** 8 servings.

Cheddar Cabbage Wedges

Unstuffed Cabbage

This recipe has all the flavor of stuffed cabbage without the work! *—Diana Filban, Cut Bank, Montana*

- 1 pound ground beef
- 1 cup chopped onion
- 1 small head cabbage, shredded
- 1 can (28 ounces) Mexican diced tomatoes, undrained
- 1 tablespoon brown sugar
- 1 tablespoon vinegar
- 1/4 teaspoon salt
- 1/8 teaspoon pepper

Hot rice

In a Dutch oven, cook beef and onion over medium heat until meat is no longer pink; drain. Stir in cabbage. Cover and cook for 5 minutes or until cabbage is crisp-tender. Stir in tomatoes, brown sugar, vinegar, salt and pepper. Cook 10 minutes longer, stirring occasionally. Serve over rice. **Yield:** 4-6 servings.

Red Cabbage Casserole

With its color and eye appeal, I like to serve this casserole on special days like Christmas or Easter when I'm cooking for a crowd. —Julie Murray
Sunderland, Ontario

   1 tablespoon shortening
   8 cups shredded red cabbage
   1 medium onion, chopped
1/2 cup lemon juice *or* vinegar
1/4 cup sugar
   1 teaspoon salt
   1 to 2 medium apples, chopped
1/4 cup red currant jelly
Lemon slices, optional

In a Dutch oven, melt shortening. Add the cabbage, onion, lemon juice, sugar and salt; mix well. Cover and cook over medium heat for 10-15 minutes or until cabbage is crisp-tender, stirring occasionally.

Add apples; cook 10-15 minutes more or until cabbage and apples are tender. Stir in jelly until melted. Garnish with lemon slices if desired. **Yield:** 8-10 servings.

Sauerkraut Stuffing

When my husband and I were married, I didn't know how to boil water. Now, many years later, there are over 900 cookbooks and counting in my collection.
—Mary Brown, Rochester, Minnesota

3/4 cup shredded raw potatoes
3/4 cup chopped onion
1/4 cup butter
   1 can (14 ounces) sauerkraut, rinsed
      and drained
   2 tablespoons minced fresh parsley
      or 2 teaspoons dried parsley flakes
1/2 teaspoon caraway seed
1/4 teaspoon salt
1/4 teaspoon pepper
   1 broiler/fryer chicken (3-1/2 to 4 pounds)
3/4 cup water
1/4 cup all-purpose flour

In a large skillet, saute the potatoes and onion in butter until onion is tender (potatoes will still be firm). Remove from the heat. Stir in sauerkraut, parsley and seasonings; mix well. Stuff chicken cav-

Reuben Baked Potatoes

ity; place on a rack in roasting pan. Roast, uncovered, at 375° for 2 hours or until chicken is tender and juices run clear.

Remove to a serving platter and keep warm. Measure 3/4 cup of the pan drippings; pour into a saucepan. Combine water and flour; add to drippings. Cook and stir until gravy boils; boil 1 minute. Serve with the chicken. **Yield:** 4 servings.

Reuben Baked Potatoes

(Pictured above)

This was a family favorite my mother made often. I still make them for potlucks. —Erika Antolic
Vancouver, Washington

   4 large baking potatoes
   2 cups finely diced cooked corned beef
   1 can (14 ounces) sauerkraut, rinsed, well
      drained and finely chopped
1/2 cup shredded Swiss cheese
   3 tablespoons sliced green onions
   1 garlic clove, minced
   1 tablespoon prepared horseradish
   1 teaspoon caraway seed
   1 package (3 ounces) cream cheese,
      softened
   3 tablespoons grated Parmesan cheese
Paprika

Bake the potatoes at 425° for 45 minutes or until tender. Cool. In a bowl, combine the corned beef, sauerkraut, Swiss cheese, onions, garlic, horseradish and caraway.

Cut potatoes in half lengthwise. Carefully scoop out potatoes, leaving shells intact. Mash potatoes with cream cheese; stir into the corned beef mixture. Mound potato mixture into the shells. Sprinkle with Parmesan cheese and paprika. Return to the oven for 25 minutes or until heated through. **Yield:** 8 servings.

Beef and Cabbage Stew

Beef and Cabbage Stew

(Pictured above)

The wonderful aroma of this stew simmering on the stove draws my family to the kitchen!
—*Sharon Downs, St. Louis, Missouri*

  1 pound ground beef
1/2 cup chopped onion
  2 cans (16 ounces *each*) kidney beans,
    rinsed and drained
  1 can (14-1/2 ounces) beef broth
  1 can (16 ounces) crushed tomatoes
  4 cups chopped cabbage
1/2 teaspoon dried basil
1/2 teaspoon dried marjoram
1/2 teaspoon dried thyme
1/2 teaspoon salt
1/8 teaspoon pepper

In a Dutch oven, cook beef and onion over medium heat until meat is no longer pink and onion is tender; drain. In a small bowl, mash 1/4 cup beans with 1/4 cup beef broth. Add to Dutch oven with remaining beans and broth, tomatoes, cabbage and seasonings. Cover and simmer for 30 minutes or until the cabbage is tender. **Yield:** 6-8 servings.

Cabbage Fruit Salad

This salad goes well with all meats—it's especially good at barbecues—and fish.
—*Florence McNulty, Montebello, California*

  4 cups shredded cabbage
  2 oranges, peeled and cut into bite-size
    pieces
  2 red apples, chopped
  1 cup seedless red grape halves
1/4 cup currants *or* raisins
1/2 cup mayonnaise
1/4 cup milk
  1 tablespoon lemon juice
  1 tablespoon sugar
1/8 teaspoon salt
1/2 cup chopped pecans, toasted

In a large bowl, toss cabbage, oranges, apples, grapes and currants; cover and refrigerate. In a small bowl, combine the mayonnaise, milk, lemon juice, sugar and salt; cover and refrigerate. Just before serving, stir dressing and pecans into salad. **Yield:** 6-8 servings.

Creamy Noodles And Cabbage

This stovetop supper is one I like to serve my family quite often. —*Gail Nero, Canton, Georgia*

  6 tablespoons butter
  1 small head cabbage, chopped
  1 medium onion, chopped
1/4 teaspoon salt
1/4 teaspoon pepper
  2 cups half-and-half cream
  1 tablespoon all-purpose flour
  1 package (12 ounces) noodles *or*
    fettuccine, cooked and drained
  1 cup (4 ounces) shredded Parmesan
    cheese
1/2 cup crumbled cooked bacon

In a Dutch oven, melt butter. Add cabbage, onion, salt and pepper. Cook and stir until vegetables are crisp-tender, about 10 minutes.

  Combine cream and flour. Add to vegetables; bring to a boil and boil 1 minute. Stir in noodles and Parmesan cheese; mix well. Pour into serving dish and sprinkle with bacon. Serve immediately. **Yield:** 10-12 servings.

Dilly Corned Beef And Cabbage

One year, when St. Patrick's Day was coming near, I knew what would happen if I served plain cabbage again—the kids would all go "yuck"! So I decided to try this recipe. It's now become a tradition.
—*June Bridges, Franklin, Indiana*

1 corned beef brisket (2-1/2 to 3-1/2 pounds)
1/4 cup honey
3 teaspoons Dijon mustard, *divided*
1 medium head cabbage (3 pounds)
2 tablespoons butter, melted
1 tablespoon minced fresh dill *or* **1 teaspoon dill weed**

Place brisket with its seasoning packet in a Dutch oven; add enough water to cover. Cover and simmer 2-1/2 hours or until tender. Remove the brisket and place on a broiling pan; reserve cooking liquid in Dutch oven.

Combine the honey and 1 teaspoon mustard; brush half over meat. Broil 4 in. from the heat for 3 minutes. Brush with the remaining honey mixture; broil 2 minutes more or until glazed.

Meanwhile, cut cabbage into eight wedges; simmer in cooking liquid for 10-15 minutes or until tender. Combine butter, dill and remaining mustard; serve over the cabbage wedges and sliced corned beef. **Yield:** 6-8 servings.

Old-Fashioned Cabbage Rolls

(Pictured below right)

It was an abundance of dill in my garden that led me to try this. My family liked the taste so much that, from then on, I made my cabbage rolls with dill.
—Florence Krantz, Bismarck, North Dakota

1 medium head cabbage (3 pounds)
1/2 pound ground beef
1/2 pound ground pork
1 can (15 ounces) tomato sauce, *divided*
1 small onion, chopped
1/2 cup uncooked long grain rice
1 tablespoon dried parsley flakes
1/2 teaspoon salt
1/2 teaspoon dill weed
1/8 teaspoon cayenne pepper
1 can (16 ounces) diced tomatoes, undrained
1/2 teaspoon sugar

Remove core from cabbage. In a large kettle or Dutch oven, cook cabbage in boiling salted water for 2-3 minutes. Remove outer leaves when softened; return to boiling water as necessary to obtain 12 leaves. Drain; remove thick center vein from leaves.

In a bowl, combine beef, pork, 1/2 cup tomato sauce, onion, rice, parsley, salt, dill and cayenne

pepper; mix well. Place about 1/4 cup meat mixture on each cabbage leaf. Fold in sides; starting at unfolded edge, roll up to completely enclose filling.

Slice the remaining cabbage; place in a large kettle or Dutch oven. Arrange the cabbage rolls seam side down over cabbage. Combine tomatoes, sugar and remaining tomato sauce; pour over the rolls. Cover and bake at 350° for 1-1/2 hours or until meat is no longer pink. **Yield:** 6-8 servings.

Barbecued Beef Sandwiches

The great thing about this recipe—especially for non-cabbage lovers!—is that you can't taste the cabbage in the meat. Yet, at the same time, it adds a nice heartiness and moistness to it.
—Denise Marshall, Bagley, Wisconsin

2 pounds beef stew meat
2 cups water
4 cups shredded cabbage
1/2 cup bottled barbecue sauce
1/2 cup ketchup
1/3 cup Worcestershire sauce
1 tablespoon prepared horseradish
1 tablespoon prepared mustard
10 hamburger *or* **other sandwich buns, split**

In a covered Dutch oven or saucepan, simmer beef in water for 1-1/2 hours or until tender. Drain cooking liquid, reserving 3/4 cup. Cool beef; shred and return to the Dutch oven.

Add the cabbage, barbecue sauce, ketchup, Worcestershire sauce, horseradish, mustard and the reserved cooking liquid. Cover and simmer for 1 hour. Serve warm in buns. **Yield:** 10 servings.

Old-Fashioned Cabbage Rolls

Southwestern Onion Rings
Onion Beef Au Jus

Chapter 14
Onions

Southwestern Onion Rings

(Pictured at left)

These light crispy onion rings are sliced thin and spiced just right with garlic powder, cayenne pepper, chili powder and cumin. My family likes them alongside grilled burgers. They're even good as leftovers.
—Tamra Kriedeman, Enderlin, North Dakota

2 large sweet onions
2-1/2 cups buttermilk
2 eggs
3 tablespoons water
1-3/4 cups all-purpose flour
2 teaspoons salt
2 teaspoons chili powder
1 to 2 teaspoons cayenne pepper
1 teaspoon sugar
1 teaspoon garlic powder
1 teaspoon ground cumin
Oil for deep-fat frying

Cut onions into 1/4-in. slices; separate into rings. Place in a bowl; cover with buttermilk and soak for 30 minutes, stirring twice.

In another bowl, beat eggs and water. In a shallow dish, combine the flour, salt, chili powder, cayenne, sugar, garlic powder and cumin. Drain onion rings; dip in egg mixture, then coat with flour mixture.

In an electric skillet or deep-fat fryer, heat 1 in. of oil to 375°. Fry onion rings, a few at a time, for 1 to 1-1/2 minutes on each side or until golden brown. Drain on paper towels. **Yield:** 8 servings.

Onion Beef Au Jus

(Pictured at left)

Garlic, onions, soy sauce and onion soup mix flavor the tender beef in these savory hot sandwiches served with a tasty rich broth for dipping. The seasoned beef makes delicious cold sandwiches, too.
—Marilyn Brown, West Union, Iowa

1 boneless beef rump roast (4 pounds)
2 tablespoons vegetable oil
2 large sweet onions, cut into 1/4-inch slices
6 tablespoons butter, softened, *divided*
5 cups water
1/2 cup soy sauce
1 envelope onion soup mix
1 garlic clove, minced
1 teaspoon browning sauce, optional
1 loaf (1 pound) French bread
1 cup (4 ounces) shredded Swiss cheese

In a Dutch oven over medium-high heat, brown roast on all sides in oil; drain. In a large skillet, saute onions in 2 tablespoons of butter until tender. Add the water, soy sauce, soup mix, garlic and browning sauce if desired. Pour over roast. Cover and bake at 325° for 2-1/2 hours or until meat is tender. Let stand for 10 minutes before slicing. Return meat to pan juices.

Slice bread in half lengthwise; cut into 3-in. sections. Spread remaining butter over bread. Place on a baking sheet. Broil 4-6 in. from the heat for 2-3 minutes or until golden brown. Top with beef and onions; sprinkle with cheese. Broil 4-6 in. from the heat for 1-2 minutes or until cheese is melted. Serve with pan juices. **Yield:** 12 servings.

Onion Pointers

Onions have a variety of natural chemicals linked to lowering blood pressure and cholesterol levels. They are also low in sodium, contain no fat, add dietary fiber and are a good source of vitamin C. *—Cathy Gilpin Alamosa, Colorado*

I save clean worn-out nylons and drop onions in the legs. I tie a knot between each onion and hang them in a cool, dry place. The onions stay nice and fresh since air can circulate around them. *—Naomi Giddis Two Buttes, Colorado*

Triple-Onion Baked Potatoes

8 cups water
3 packages (10 ounces *each*) fresh pearl
  onions
1 tablespoon butter
1 tablespoon vegetable oil
1-1/2 cups cranberry juice
1/2 teaspoon salt
1 can (16 ounces) jellied cranberry sauce
1/2 teaspoon lemon juice

In a large saucepan, bring water to a boil. Add onions; boil for 3 minutes. Drain and rinse in cold water; peel.

In a large skillet, cook onions in butter and oil over medium heat until lightly browned, about 5 minutes. Add cranberry juice and salt. Bring to a boil. Reduce heat to medium-low; cover and cook just until onions are tender. Add cranberry sauce and lemon juice; cook and stir until mixture is thick and syrupy. **Yield:** 6 servings.

Triple-Onion Baked Potatoes

(Pictured above)

These potatoes feature a rich filling of onions, bacon, sour cream and cheese. I like to serve them with baked ham. —Char Shanahan, Schererville, Indiana

4 large baking potatoes
1 pound sliced bacon, diced
1/2 cup finely chopped red onion
1/2 cup finely chopped yellow onion
1/2 cup sour cream
2 tablespoons milk
1 cup diced American cheese
1/2 cup shredded cheddar cheese
4 green onions, finely sliced

Bake potatoes at 400° for 1 hour or until tender. Meanwhile, in a large skillet, cook the bacon over medium heat until crisp; remove to paper towels. Drain, reserving 1 tablespoon drippings. In the drippings, saute red and yellow onions until tender; set aside.

When cool enough to handle, cut potatoes in half lengthwise. Scoop out pulp, leaving an 1/8-in. shell. In a mixing bowl, beat pulp, sour cream and milk until creamy. Stir in sauteed onions, American cheese and 1 cup bacon. Spoon into shells.

Place on a baking sheet. Bake at 400° for 25 minutes. Sprinkle with cheddar cheese, green onions and remaining bacon. Bake 5-10 minutes longer or until cheese is melted. **Yield:** 8 servings.

Garlic-Onion Tomato Pizza

You won't miss the traditional tomato sauce when you bite into a slice of this pizza—it is absolutely delicious! —Tammy Thomas, Sheboygan, Wisconsin

2 teaspoons cornmeal
2 packages (1/4 ounce *each*) active
  dry yeast
2 cups warm water (110° to 115°)
5 to 6 cups all-purpose flour
4 teaspoons plus 1 tablespoon olive oil,
  divided
1 teaspoon salt
2 medium sweet onions, thinly sliced
8 large garlic cloves, halved
6 to 8 plum tomatoes, cut lengthwise into
  eighths and seeded
2 tablespoons dried oregano
2 tablespoons dried parsley flakes
Pepper to taste
1-1/2 cups (6 ounces) shredded mozzarella
  cheese
1/4 cup grated Romano cheese

Sprinkle cornmeal evenly over two greased 14-in. pizza pans; set aside. In a bowl, dissolve yeast in water; add 4-1/2 cups flour, 4 teaspoons oil and salt; beat until smooth. Add enough remaining flour to form a soft dough.

Turn onto a floured surface; knead until smooth and elastic, 6-8 minutes. Place in a greased bowl; turn once to grease top. Cover and let rise in a warm place until doubled, about 1 hour.

Punch dough down; divide in half. Press each portion into prepared pans. Prick dough with a fork. Bake at 450° for 4-5 minutes. Broil onions and garlic in batches 3-4 in. from the heat until softened and lightly browned. Broil tomato slices for 2

Cranberry Pearl Onions

This unusual combination of pearl onions and cranberries is surprisingly delicious. There's plenty of thick, dark red sauce, and the onions have a sweet-tangy taste. —Lesley Tragesser, Charleston, Missouri

Taste of Home's Garden-Fresh Recipes

minutes on each side. Finely chop garlic.

Arrange onions, garlic and tomatoes over crusts. Sprinkle with oregano, parsley, pepper and cheeses; drizzle with remaining oil. Bake at 450° for 8-9 minutes or until cheese is melted. **Yield:** 2 pizzas (8 slices each).

Marinated Onion Salad

Everyone knows how sweet onions flavor all kinds of food, but in this recipe, they take center stage!
—Michelle Wrightsman, Linwood, Kansas

3 medium sweet onions, thinly sliced
4 cups boiling water
4 medium cucumbers, thinly sliced
1 cup (8 ounces) plain yogurt
1 teaspoon lemon juice
1-1/2 teaspoons salt
1/8 teaspoon pepper
Dash Worcestershire sauce
Dash vinegar
1 teaspoon dill weed, optional
2 tablespoons minced fresh parsley

Separate onions into rings and place in a large bowl; pour water over onions. Let stand 1 minute; drain. Add cucumbers. In a small bowl, combine the yogurt, lemon juice, salt, pepper, Worcestershire sauce, vinegar and dill if desired; mix well.

Pour over onion mixture; toss to coat. Chill until serving. Sprinkle with parsley. Serve with a slotted spoon. **Yield:** 16-20 servings.

Vidalia Casserole

Georgia is famous for the sweet onions grown in the Vidalia area. My family looks forward to the time these onions are available to use in salads and casseroles.
—Libby Bigger, Dunwoody, Georgia

4 to 5 Vidalia *or* sweet onions, sliced 1/4 inch thick
1/4 cup butter
1/4 cup sour cream
3/4 cup grated Parmesan cheese
10 butter-flavored crackers, crushed

In a skillet over medium heat, saute onions in butter until tender. Remove from the heat; stir in sour cream. Spoon half into a greased 1-qt. baking dish. Sprinkle with cheese. Top with remaining onion mixture and crackers. Bake, uncovered, at 350° for 20-25 minutes. **Yield:** 4-6 servings.

Meaty Stuffed Onions

(Pictured below)

I won a prize for this recipe in a contest sponsored by our local newspaper. I got it from my mother-in-law, who's originally from Italy. —Lorraine Grasso
Allentown, Pennsylvania

4 large sweet onions
1 pound ground beef
1/2 pound bulk pork sausage
1 package (10 ounces) frozen chopped spinach, thawed and drained
5 slices day-old bread, crumbled
1/2 to 2/3 cup beef broth
1/2 cup grated Parmesan cheese
1 egg, beaten
1 tablespoon minced fresh parsley
1/2 teaspoon salt
1/4 teaspoon pepper
1/8 teaspoon ground nutmeg

Peel onions and cut 1/2 in. off tops and bottoms. Place onions in a large saucepan. Cover with boiling water. Cook until tender, about 20 minutes; drain. Cool slightly. Carefully remove inside layers of onion, separating into eight individual shells (refrigerate remaining onion for another use). Drain on paper towels.

In a skillet, cook beef and sausage over medium heat until no longer pink; drain. Add spinach; cook and stir for 2 minutes. Remove from the heat; stir in the remaining ingredients. Spoon into the onion shells. Place in a greased 13-in. x 9-in. x 2-in. baking pan. Bake, uncovered, at 350° for 15-20 minutes or until heated through and lightly browned. **Yield:** 8 servings.

Meaty Stuffed Onions

Onion Brie Appetizers

(Pictured below)

Guests will think you spent hours preparing these cute appetizers, but they're really easy to assemble, using purchased puff pastry. And the tasty combination of Brie, caramelized onions and caraway is terrific.
—Carole Resnick, Cleveland, Ohio

- **2 medium onions, thinly sliced**
- **3 tablespoons butter**
- **2 tablespoons brown sugar**
- **1/2 teaspoon white wine vinegar**
- **1 sheet frozen puff pastry, thawed**
- **4 ounces Brie *or* Camembert, rind removed, softened**
- **1 to 2 teaspoons caraway seeds**
- **1 egg**
- **2 teaspoons water**

In a large skillet, cook the onions, butter, brown sugar and vinegar over medium-low heat until onions are golden brown, stirring frequently. Remove with a slotted spoon; cool to room temperature.

On a lightly floured surface, roll puff pastry into an 11-in. x 8-in. rectangle. Spread Brie over pastry. Cover with the onions; sprinkle with caraway seeds. Roll up one long side to the middle of the dough; roll up the other side so the two rolls meet in the center. Using a serrated knife, cut into 1/2-in. slices. Place on parchment paper-lined baking sheets; flatten to 1/4-in. thickness. Refrigerate for 15 minutes.

In a small bowl, beat egg and water; brush over slices. Bake at 375° for 12-14 minutes or until puffed and golden brown. Serve warm. **Yield:** 1-1/2 dozen.

Onion Brie Appetizers

Onion Cream Soup

My whole family loves this hearty soup, especially on cool autumn evenings. It's rich and creamy with a mild onion-cheese flavor. When I need an easy dinner, I stir up this soup and serve it with warm crusty bread and a crisp salad.
—Janice Hemond
Lincoln, Rhode Island

- **2 cups thinly sliced sweet onions**
- **6 tablespoons butter, *divided***
- **1 can (14-1/2 ounces) chicken broth**
- **2 teaspoons chicken bouillon granules**
- **1/4 teaspoon pepper**
- **3 tablespoons all-purpose flour**
- **1-1/2 cups milk**
- **1/4 cup diced process cheese (Velveeta)**
- **Shredded cheddar cheese and minced fresh parsley**

In a large skillet, cook onions in 3 tablespoons butter over medium-low heat until tender. Add the broth, bouillon and pepper; bring to a boil. Remove from the heat.

In a large saucepan, melt the remaining butter. Stir in flour until smooth; gradually add milk. Bring to a boil; cook and stir for 1-2 minutes or until thickened. Reduce heat; add process cheese and onion mixture. Cook and stir until heated through and cheese is melted. Garnish with cheddar cheese and parsley. **Yield:** 4 servings.

Onion Pie

Our area has the right kind of soil for growing beautiful onions, so we always have plenty to enjoy. My mother got this recipe 30 years ago and said it originated in a Pennsylvania Dutch kitchen.
—Marian Benthin, Apalachin, New York

- **1-1/3 cups biscuit/baking mix**
- **1 teaspoon rubbed sage**
- **1/2 teaspoon salt**
- **4 to 5 tablespoons milk**
- **FILLING:**
- **5 cups thinly sliced onions (about 5 medium)**
- **2 tablespoons vegetable oil**
- **1/2 teaspoon salt**
- **1 egg**
- **1 cup half-and-half cream**

In a bowl, combine the biscuit mix, sage and salt. Add enough milk until mixture holds together. Press onto the bottom and up the sides of a 9-in. pie plate; set aside. In a large skillet, saute onions in oil until tender. Sprinkle with salt. Spoon into crust. In a bowl, beat egg and cream; pour over onions.

Bake, uncovered, at 375° for 15 minutes. Reduce heat to 325°. Bake 25-30 minutes longer or until a knife inserted near the center comes out clean. **Yield:** 6-8 servings.

Creamy Sweet Onions

Well coated with a tangy sour cream and celery seed dressing, these sweet-sour onions really dress up a juicy burger. My sister likes to serve them as a side salad when our family gets together in summer up at the lakes. —Ethel Lowey, Fort Frances, Ontario

5 large white onions, thinly sliced
2-1/4 cups sugar
1-1/2 cups cider vinegar
1-1/2 cups water
    4 teaspoons salt
    1 cup (8 ounces) sour cream
    3 tablespoons mayonnaise
1/4 teaspoon celery seed
Salt and pepper to taste

Place the onions in a large bowl. In a saucepan, combine the sugar, vinegar, water and salt. Bring to a boil; pour over onions. Cover and refrigerate overnight.

Drain onions, discarding liquid. In a bowl, combine the sour cream, mayonnaise, celery seed, salt and pepper; mix well. Add onions and toss to coat. **Yield:** 4 cups.

Amish Onion Cake

(Pictured above right)

This rich, moist bread with an onion-poppy seed topping is a wonderful break from your everyday bread routine. You can serve it with any meat, and it's a nice accompaniment to soup or salad. I've made it many times and have often been asked to share the recipe. —Mitzi Sentiff, Alexandria, Virginia

3 to 4 medium onions, chopped
2 cups cold butter, *divided*
1 tablespoon poppy seeds
1-1/2 teaspoons salt
1-1/2 teaspoons paprika
    1 teaspoon coarsely ground pepper
    4 cups all-purpose flour
1/2 cup cornstarch
    1 tablespoon baking powder
    1 tablespoon sugar
    1 tablespoon brown sugar
    5 eggs
3/4 cup milk
3/4 cup sour cream

Amish Onion Cake

In a large skillet, cook onions in 1/2 cup butter over low heat for 10 minutes. Stir in the poppy seeds, salt, paprika and pepper; cook until golden brown, stirring occasionally. Remove from the heat; set aside. In a bowl, combine the flour, cornstarch, baking powder and sugars. Cut in 1-1/4 cups butter until mixture resembles coarse crumbs.

Melt the remaining butter. In a bowl, whisk the eggs, milk, sour cream and melted butter. Make a well in dry ingredients; stir in egg mixture just until moistened. Spread into a greased 10-in. springform pan. Spoon onion mixture over the dough.

Place pan on a baking sheet. Bake at 350° for 35-40 minutes or until a toothpick inserted near the center comes out clean. Serve warm. **Yield:** 10-12 servings.

Maple Baked Onions

I created this side dish to make use of the great maple syrup we have here in Vermont. My family loves this recipe, and it's so easy to prepare. —Donna Kurant
West Rutland, Vermont

6 large sweet onions, sliced 1/2 inch thick
1/3 cup maple syrup
1/4 cup butter, melted

Layer onions in a greased 13-in. x 9-in. x 2-in. baking dish. Combine syrup and butter; pour over onions. Bake, uncovered, at 425° for 40-45 minutes or until tender. **Yield:** 8-10 servings.

Guide to Vegetables

When you're looking for creative ways to vary the family menu, vegetables certainly are the place to start. Pretty, tasty and nutritious, vegetables can be prepared in minutes using the basic methods of boiling or steaming, or they can be teamed with other ingredients to make unique flavor combinations as they stew or bake.

Cook them until they are crisp-tender or as recipes direct. Keep in mind that cooking times will vary due to the size, freshness and ripeness of the vegetable.

ASPARAGUS

Asparagus have a slender light green stalk with a tightly closed bud at the top. They are most often served cooked as a side dish but can be enjoyed raw on vegetable platters.

Buying tips:
Available mainly from February until late June. Peak months are April and May. Buy small, straight stalks with tightly closed, compact tips. The spears should be smooth and round. Stalks should have a bright green color, while the tips may have a slight lavender tint.

Storage tips:
Keep unwashed asparagus in a sealed plastic bag in the refrigerator crisper drawer for up to 4 days.

Preparation tips:
Soak asparagus stalks in cold water to clean. Snap off the stalk ends as far down as they will easily break when gently bent, or cut off the tough white portion. (See photo at left.)

If stalks are large, use a vegetable peeler to gently peel the tough area of the stalk from the end to just below the tip. If tips are large, scrape off scales with a knife.

Cooking tips:
To boil: Place whole asparagus in a skillet or cut asparagus in a saucepan. Add 1/2 in. of water and bring to a boil. Reduce heat; cover and simmer for 3-5 minutes or until crisp-tender. Drain. *To steam:* Place asparagus in a basket over 1 in. of boiling water in a saucepan. Cover; steam for about 5 minutes or until crisp-tender.

Yields: 1 pound of asparagus (about 14 spears) equals 2 cups cut
1 pound of asparagus serves 4

BEANS

Green and wax beans, also know as string beans, are members of the legume family. Green and wax beans may be used interchangeably in recipes and are known for their mild flavor and general appeal.

Buying tips:
Available year-round. Peak months are from July to October. Buy brightly colored, straight, smooth pods that are unblemished. Beans should be crisp and have a firm, velvety feel. Seeds inside the bean should be small.

Storage tips:
Store unwashed beans in a sealed plastic bag or covered container in the refrigerator crisper drawer for up to 3 days.

Green beans **Wax beans**

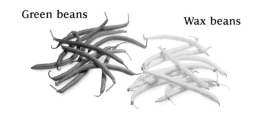

Preparation tips:
Snap off the stem end of the bean and the other end if desired. Leave whole or cut into 1-in. pieces.

Cooking tips:
To boil: Place beans in a saucepan and cover with water; bring to a boil. Cook, uncovered, for 8-10 minutes or until crisp-tender. Drain. *To steam:* Place beans in a basket over 1 in. of boiling water in a saucepan. Cover; steam for 8-10 minutes or until crisp-tender.

Yields: 1 pound of beans equals about 4 cups cut
1 pound of beans serves 4 to 6

BROCCOLI

A member of the cauliflower family, broccoli has pale green thick stalks with tightly packed dark green heads (florets) with a slight purple tint. Stalks and florets are eaten raw or cooked.

Buying tips:
Available year-round. Select firm but tender stalks with compact, dark green or slightly purplish florets.

Storage tips:
Keep unwashed broccoli in an open plastic bag in the refrigerator crisper drawer up to 4 days.

Preparation tips:
Remove larger leaves and tough ends of lower stalks. Wash broccoli. If using whole spears, cut lengthwise into 1-in.-wide pieces; stalks may also be peeled for more even cooking. If using florets, cut 1/4 in. to 1/2 in. below heads; discard stalks.

Cooking tips:
To boil: Place broccoli in a saucepan; add 1 in. of water. Bring to a boil. Reduce heat; cover and simmer for 5-8 minutes or until crisp-tender. Drain. *To steam:* Place broccoli in a basket over 1 in. of boiling water in a saucepan. Cover; steam for 5-8 minutes or until crisp-tender and bright green in color.

Yields: 1 pound of broccoli equals 3-1/2 cups florets
1 pound of broccoli serves 3 to 4

CABBAGE

Cabbage is a fleshy-leafed member of the mustard family that ranges in color from white to green to deep reddish-purple. Heads are dense and heavy. Serve raw in salads or use cooked in entrees and side dishes. Cabbage is often shredded for slaw and sliced or cut into wedges for cooking.

Green cabbage

Red cabbage

Buying tips:
Available year-round. For green cabbage, buy round, compact, solid heads that seem heavy for their size. Cabbage heads will vary in size, but the leaves should be tight, smooth and unblemished. Red cabbage heads are not as compact as green cabbage heads. The color should be a reddish-purple.

Storage tips:
Place unwashed cabbage in a sealed plastic bag in the refrigerator crisper drawer for up to 7 days.

Preparation tips:
Wash head. Trim center core to within 1/4 in. of leaves; remove any discolored, damaged or tough outer leaves from head.

Cooking tips:
To boil: Place cabbage wedges or slices in a saucepan; add 1 in. of water. Bring to a boil. Reduce heat; cover and simmer until crisp-tender (3-5 minutes for slices or 6-8 minutes for wedges). Drain. *To steam:* Place cabbage wedges or slices in a basket over 1 in. of boiling water in a saucepan. Cover; steam until crisp-tender (6-8 minutes for slices or 15 minutes for wedges).

Yields: 3 pounds of cabbage (1 large head) equals
14 to 16 cups shredded (uncooked)
3-1/2 cups of raw cabbage equals 2-1/2
cups cooked slices
1 pound of cabbage serves 3

CARROTS

Carrots are a long, slender root vegetable related to the parsnip that have a distinctive orange color. Smaller varieties, called baby carrots, are also available.

Buying tips:
Available year-round. Buy crisp firm, smooth, well-shaped carrots with deep orange color. Smaller carrots are tender and sweet. Carrots sold in bunches with fern-like green tops are fresher but not always available in the market.

Storage tips:
Trim tops and roots when present. Store unwashed unpeeled carrots in a sealed plastic bag in the refrigerator crisper drawer for 1 to 2 weeks.

Preparation tips:
Young carrots may be used unpeeled if they are well scrubbed. Larger carrots should be thinly peeled with a vegetable peeler.

Cooking tips:
To boil: Place sliced or whole baby carrots in a saucepan; add 1 in. of water. Bring to a boil. Reduce heat; cover and simmer until crisp-tender (7-9 minutes for slices or 10-15 minutes for baby carrots). Drain. *To steam:* Place whole or sliced carrots in a basket over 1 in. of boiling water in a saucepan. Cover; steam until crisp-tender (12-15 minutes for whole carrots or 8-10 minutes for cut carrots).

Yields: 1 pound of carrots (6 to 7 medium) equals 3 to 3-1/2 cups sliced (uncooked)
2 medium carrots equals 1 cup sliced or shredded
1 pound of carrots serves 4

CAULIFLOWER

This snowy-white vegetable has a flower-like appearance and a mild cabbage-like flavor. Cauliflower can be eaten raw or cooked.

Buying tips:
Available year-round. Peak months are October through March. Buy firm, solid white or creamy-colored heads that feel heavy for their size. The florets should be clean and tightly packed and the surrounding jacket leaves fresh and green.

Storage tips:
Place unwashed cauliflower in an open plastic bag in the refrigerator crisper drawer for up to 4 days.

Preparation tips:
Trim off leaves. Remove base stem at an angle so the core comes out in a cone and the head remains intact. Separate into florets if desired.

Cooking tips:

To boil: Place cauliflower florets in a saucepan; add 1 in. of water. Bring to a boil. Reduce heat; cover and simmer 5-10 minutes or until crisp-tender. Drain. *To steam:* Place cauliflower in a basket over 1 in. of boiling water in a saucepan. Cover; steam until crisp-tender (15-20 minutes for head, 5-12 minutes for florets). (See photo above.)

Yields: 1-1/2 pounds of cauliflower (about 1 head), trimmed, equals 3 cups florets
1-1/2 pounds of cauliflower serves 4

CORN ON THE COB

Also known as sweet corn, this vegetable is available with bright yellow or white kernels or a mix of both. Corn on the cob is served cooked with silk and husks removed. Cooked kernels can be cut from the cob and used in recipes in place of canned or frozen corn.

Buying tips:
Available May through August. Peak months are July and August. Select corn that has fresh green, tightly closed husks with dark brown, dry (but not brittle) silk. The stem should be moist, but not chalky, yellow or discolored. Ears should have plump, tender,  small kernels in tight rows up to the tip. Kernels should be firm enough to resist slight pressure. A fresh kernel will spurt "milk" if punctured.

Storage tips:
Keep unshucked ears in opened plastic bags in the

Taste of Home's Garden-Fresh Recipes

refrigerator crisper drawer and use within 1 day.

Preparation tips:
If boiling or steaming, remove husk by pulling the husks down the ear; break off the undeveloped tip. Trim stem. Pull out silk between kernel rows or remove with a dry vegetable brush; rinse in cold water.

Cooking tips:
To boil: Drop shucked ears into a large kettle of rapidly boiling unsalted water. Cover; return to a boil and cook for 3-5 minutes or until tender. Drain. *To roast:* Pull back husk but don't remove; remove silk. Replace husk and tie with string at the top. Soak corn for at least 1 hour in cold water. Remove from water; grill over high heat for 20-25 minutes, turning frequently.

Yields: 6 ears of corn equals about 3 cups of kernels
1 ear of corn (1/2 cup kernels) serves 1

ONIONS

White onion

Green onions

Yellow onion

Red onion

A member of the lily family, onions can be green, white, yellow or red with flavor ranging from sharp when eaten raw to mild and sweet when cooked.

Buying tips:
Available year-round. Green onions (also known as scallions) should have bright green tops with white bulbs and short roots. All other onions should have a dry, smooth papery skin. They should be unblemished, hard and globe-shaped with small necks. Avoid moist, blemished or sprouting onions. White onions have the mildest flavor. Yellow onions are the most common.

Storage tips:
Place unwashed green onions in a sealed plastic bag in the refrigerator crisper drawer for up to 5 days. All other onions should be stored in a net bag or open basket in a dry, dark, cool place for up to 4 weeks.

Preparation tips:
For green onions, wash and cut root end. Cut off green tops, leaving about 3 in. For all other onions, peel loose layers of skin and cut onions just prior to cooking. Red or purple onions are used uncooked because the color fades as it cooks.

Cooking tips:
To saute: Heat 2 tablespoons of butter or oil in a skillet over medium-high heat. Saute sliced or chopped onion until translucent. *To bake:* Place a large onion in an ungreased baking dish; add 1/4 in. of water. Cover and bake at 350° for 40-50 minutes or until tender.

Yields: 1 green onion equals 2 tablespoons sliced
1 small onion equals 1/3 cup chopped
1 medium onion equals 1/2 cup chopped
1 large onion equals 1 cup chopped

PEPPERS

Sweet bell peppers

Green pepper

Yellow pepper

Red pepper

Classified as a fruit, sweet bell peppers are enjoyed as a vegetable. They can range in color from dark green and dark purple to bright yellow and vibrant red. Sweet peppers are mild in flavor and enhance hot and cold dishes alike.

Buying tips:
Available year-round. Peak months are March through October. Buy firm, glossy, bright-colored peppers that are unblemished and have smooth skins. Bell peppers should be relatively heavy in weight.

Storage tips:
Keep unwashed bell peppers in the refrigerator crisper drawer for up to 1 week.

Preparation tips:
Bell peppers may be left whole, chopped or cut into slices or rings. Wash; remove stems, seeds and membranes (ribs).

Cooking tips:

To steam: Place whole seeded bell peppers in a basket over 1 in. of boiling water in a saucepan. Cover; steam for 8-10 minutes or until crisp-tender. Use this technique to prepare peppers for stuffing. *To saute:* Heat 1-2 tablespoons of oil in a skillet. Saute bell pepper strips or pieces for 3-5 minutes or until crisp-tender.

Follow individual recipe directions for cooking the many varieties of chili peppers.

Yield: 1 pound of bell peppers (3 medium) equals 4 cups thinly sliced

POTATOES

Known as a tuberous vegetable, potatoes are round or elongated with smooth edible skins that range in color from brown or red to white or yellow-gold. Small potatoes that are fresh from the garden and have never been placed in storage are called new potatoes.

Sweet potato

Round potato

Russet potato

Red potato

White potato

New potato

Buying tips:

White and red potatoes are available year-round. Peak months are spring and early summer for new potatoes and August to February for other varieties. Buy well-shaped, firm potatoes that are free from cuts, decay, blemishes or green discoloration under the skin. Avoid sprouted or shriveled potatoes.

Sweet potatoes (sometimes called yams) are available year-round. The peak month is November. Look for well-shaped potatoes, free of blemishes and large knots. Skins that are darker tend to be sweeter and moister.

Storage tips:

Store potatoes in a basket, net bag or paper bag in a dry, dark, cool well-ventilated area for up to 2 weeks; do not refrigerate.

Preparation tips:

Scrub with a vegetable brush. Remove eyes or sprouts. When working with large quantities of potatoes, peel and place in cold water to prevent browning.

Cooking tips for white or red potatoes:

To boil: Use red, white, yellow-gold or new potatoes. Cut large potatoes into quarters or chunks. Place in a saucepan; cover with water. Cover and bring to a boil. Cook until tender, 15-30 minutes; drain well. *To steam:* Place potato chunks in a basket over 1 in. of boiling water in a saucepan. Cover and steam until tender, 15-30 minutes. *To bake:* Use a russet potato. Pierce potato skins several times with a fork. (See photo above right.) Bake directly on oven rack at 375° for 1 hour or until potato feels soft when it's gently squeezed. If you prefer a soft-skinned baked potato, wrap in foil or rub with oil before baking it.

Cooking tips for sweet potatoes:

To boil: Place whole scrubbed potatoes in a large kettle and cover with water. Cover and boil gently until potatoes can easily be pierced with the tip of a sharp knife, about 30-45 minutes. Drain and peel as soon as they are cool enough to handle. *To bake:* Pierce potatoes several times with a fork. Bake directly on oven rack at 400° for about 45 minutes or until soft when gently squeezed. Place a piece of foil under potatoes to catch drips.

Yields: 1 pound russet potatoes equals about 3 medium
1 pound small new potatoes equals 8 to 10 (about 3 servings)
1 pound potatoes equals 2-1/4 cups diced or sliced
1 medium white, red or sweet potato serves 1
1 pound sweet potatoes (3 medium) equals about 2 cups mashed

Taste of Home's Garden-Fresh Recipes

SQUASH

Summer squash, a member of the gourd family, are soft-skinned, tender and quick-cooking. Varieties include pattypan, sunburst, yellow crookneck and zucchini. All contain small soft edible seeds and edible skins. Summer squash can be eaten raw or cooked.

Winter squash, also a member of the gourd family, are dense vegetables with a hard shell and large seeds. Varieties include acorn, butternut, spaghetti and turban. Winter squash is always cooked before serving.

Summer Squash

Zucchini
Yellow crookneck
Sunburst
Pattypan

Winter Squash

Butternut
Spaghetti
Acorn
Turban

Buying tips:
Summer squash are available year-round. Peak months are May through August. Buy squash that have glossy, smooth and firm but tender skins. Small squash are more tender and flavorful.

Winter squash are available year-round. Peak months are October through December. Buy squash that have a coarse, hard rind. The squash should feel heavy for its size.

Storage tips:
Keep unwashed summer squash in a sealed plastic bag in the refrigerator crisper drawer for up to 4 days.

Keep unwashed winter squash in a dry, cool, well-ventilated place for up to 4 weeks.

Preparation tips:
Wash summer squash, but do not peel. Remove stem and blossom ends. Serve pattypan squash whole if young (1 to 2 in.). Slice zucchini and yellow squash into 1/2-in. circles.

Wash winter squash. Trim stem; cut into halves or individual portions. Remove seeds and stringy portions. Acorn squash can be cut into decorative rings and steamed or baked. (See photo at right.)

Cooking tips for summer squash:
To steam: Place squash in a basket over 1 in. of boiling water in a saucepan. Cover; steam for 5 minutes or until crisp-tender. *To saute:* Heat several tablespoons of butter or oil in a skillet. Saute squash over medium-high heat for 5 minutes or until crisp-tender.

Cooking tips for winter squash:
To steam: Peel and dice squash. Place in a basket over 1 in. of boiling water in a saucepan. Cover; steam for 15-20 minutes or until tender. *To bake:* Cut squash in half or quarters if large; place cut side down in a greased baking dish. Bake, uncovered, at 350° for 45-60 minutes or until tender.

Yields for summer squash:
    1 pound of squash equals 4 cups grated or
      3-1/2 cups sliced
    1 pound of squash serves 3 to 4

Yields for winter squash:
    1 pound of squash equals 2 cups cooked mashed
    1 pound of squash serves 2

TOMATOES

Classified as a fruit, but used as a vegetable, tomatoes are smooth-skinned, round or pear-shaped and bright red or yellow when ripe. They are eaten raw or cooked.

Common red tomato

Plum tomatoes

Pear-shaped tomatoes

Cherry tomatoes

Buying tips:
Available year-round. Peak months are June through October for local vine-ripened tomatoes. Buy nicely ripe, rich-colored, well-shaped tomatoes that are slightly soft. Tomatoes should be free of blemishes.

Storage tips:
Keep unwashed tomatoes at room temperature for 1 to 2 days. Keep out of direct sunlight.

Preparation tips:
Wash and core tomatoes. To remove peel, place tomato in boiling water for 30 seconds. Immediately dip in ice water. Remove skin with a sharp paring knife. (See photos at right.)

To seed a tomato, cut in half and gently squeeze the tomato over a bowl. Use a small spoon to remove remaining seeds.

Cooking tips:
To broil: Place tomato halves 3-4 in. from the heat. Broil just until heated through or when the skin begins to split. *To bake:* Place tomato halves cut side up in a greased baking dish. Season as desired. Bake at 400° for 8-15 minutes or until just heated through and skin begins to wrinkle.

Yield: 1 pound of tomatoes (about 3 medium) equals 1-1/2 cups peeled seeded pulp

Guide to Common Herbs

Basil: Known for its licorice-like flavor, basil leaves are used fresh or dried. Probably most used in tomato or pasta dishes, basil also adds flavor to dips, soups, marinated salads, vegetables, stews, fish, beef, salad dressings, poultry and cheese dishes.

Cilantro: Also known as coriander or Chinese parsley, the zesty-flavored green leaves of this herb are used fresh in Mexican-style dishes. Cilantro leaves add distinctive flavor to salsas, Southwestern-style appetizers, dips, sauces, chili, pesto and rice and bean dishes. Cilantro is best added to dishes just before serving to retain its fresh flavor.

Marjoram: Used fresh or dried, marjoram's green leaves have a strong sweet aroma much like oregano. Add to meat, poultry, fish, egg, homemade sausage and vegetable dishes. It's especially good with Italian-style foods.

Oregano: The dark green leaves of oregano are used fresh or dried in Italian, Mexican and Greek dishes. Oregano flavors soups, stews, chili, poultry, ground beef, seafood, marinades, salad dressings, sauces, hot or cold pasta dishes and pizza.

Parsley: Available in curly and flat-leaf varieties, fresh parsley adds a refreshing flavor and spark of green garnish to soups, salads, salad dressings, sauces, fish, poultry, poultry stuffings and potato, grain, bean and pasta dishes. Flat-leaf or Italian parsley has a stronger flavor than the traditional curly variety. Dried parsley is mild in flavor and color.

Rosemary: Known for its needle-like leaves, rosemary has a distinctive fragrant evergreen scent and bold flavor. Fresh or dried rosemary complements lamb, pork, poultry, marinades, potato dishes, herb butters and homemade savory breads.

Tarragon: Tarragon's long slender leaves have a mild licorice-like flavor and are used fresh or dried. Tarragon flavors chicken, poultry marinades, pasta salads, potato salads, vegetables, sauces, salad dressings, fish and egg dishes.

Taste of Home's Garden-Fresh Recipes

INDEX

✓ Recipe includes Nutritional Analysis and Diabetic Exchanges.

✓ Recipe includes Nutritional Analysis and Diabetic Exchanges.

✓ Recipe includes Nutritional Analysis and Diabetic Exchanges.

✓ Recipe includes Nutritional Analysis and Diabetic Exchanges.

Taste of Home's Garden-Fresh Recipes